Alternatives to Exclusion from School

School of Educational Studies

Alternatives to Exclusion from School

Pamela Munn, Gwynedd Lloyd and
Mairi Ann Cullen

P·C·P
Paul Chapman
Publishing Ltd

To Margaret Johnstone, a good friend and colleague who contributed substantially to the research as a member of the team. The book is a belated present on her retirement.

First published 2000

 Paul Chapman Publishing Ltd
A SAGE Publications Company
6 Bonhill Street
London EC2A 4PU

SAGE Publications Inc.
2455 Teller Road
Thousand Oaks, California 91320

SAGE Publications India Pvt Ltd
32, M-Block Market
Greater Kailash-I
New Delhi 110 048

British Cataloguing in Publication Data
A catalogue record for this book is available from the British Library

ISBN 1 85396 456 5
ISBN 1 85396 457 3 (pbk)

Library of Congress catalog card number available

Typeset by Anneset, Weston-super-Mare, Somerset
Printed and bound in Great Britain by Athenaeum Press, Gateshead

Contents

Notes on the Authors

Pamela Munn is Professor of Curriculum Research and Associate Dean (Postgraduate) in the Faculty of Education, University of Edinburgh. She has led major research studies on school discipline, exclusion and truancy. She has published widely in this area and has been associated with a number of developments aimed at helping schools share their experience of positive approaches to discipline. She is currently the director of the Scottish Schools Ethos Network and of the Anti-Bullying Network and has been a consultant to the Scottish Office on New Community Schools. She has recently returned to Edinburgh from a three month stay at the Graduate School of Education, University of Tokyo, where she was visiting Professor of Education.

Gwynedd Lloyd is Senior Lecturer in the Department of Equity Studies and Special Education at the University of Edinburgh. She has researched, written about and worked with children in difficulty. Recent publications have included articles on counselling skills in education, on the exclusion of Traveller pupils, on gender and emotional and behavioural difficulties and on inclusion and ADHD.

Mairi Ann Cullen is a Senior Research Officer in the Department of Professional and Curriculum Studies at the National Foundation for Educational Research. She has worked on, and written about, a number of research projects relating to special educational needs, disaffection/disengagement and exclusion from school. Most recently, she has led research projects on alternative curriculum programmes for 14–16-year-olds in England and Wales and on the delivery of the curriculum to disengaged young people in Scotland. She has also worked in, and carried out research on, adult and community education.

Introduction

Exclusion from school is a major concern in the United Kingdom and ways of preventing it feature strongly in the Labour government's commitment to tackle social exclusion more generally. Exclusion from school can be *permanent*, the excluded pupil being refused readmission and having to seek alternative provision; or *fixed term* where readmission after a specific time is granted provided certain conditions are met; or *informal* where a pupil is sent home but no record of this is kept. Most research has focused on permanent exclusions, on mapping the characteristics of permanently excluded pupils and on the impact of exclusions on pupils and their families. Research has also highlighted the estimated financial costs of permanent exclusion.

This book grew out of a research project, funded by the Scottish Office, to take a broader look at exclusion. The project was to map the extent of exclusions and gather information on excluded pupils but it was also to explore in-school alternatives to exclusion. This aspect of the work was conducted through case studies of 'matched pairs' of schools in terms of size and the socio-economic status of pupils attending, but different in their use of exclusion. A starting point of the book, then, was the wish to share findings on in-school alternatives to exclusion within and beyond Scotland.

An important message of the book is that schools and teachers can make a difference to young people's emotional and social development as well as to their cognitive-intellectual development. They can improve pupils' self-esteem, can give confidence and can prevent learning problems becoming behaviour problems. For many children with difficulties in their families or communities, school can be a safe and supportive refuge. The importance of school to children who are being looked after out of their original families has often been stated, although equally the educational failure of such pupils is documented.

It is important to make clear that children's personal and social development takes place through the everyday operation of the normal curriculum and, indeed, all children may find opportunities to explore difficult aspects of their lives through drama, art, free or structured play and through typical subjects on the timetable as well as through slots labelled personal and social development or specialist provision.

School, however, is much more than the subjects on the timetable and a focus of the research was on the hidden curriculum or school ethos as a vehicle for preventing exclusion as well as on understanding particular in-school alternatives. School routines, values and practices send messages about who and what is valued and about the expectations of the kind of relationships that will exist between teachers and pupils. The importance of school ethos in creating a positive approach to school discipline is discussed in Chapter 4.

The book is more than a report of the project in three ways. First, it goes beyond in-school alternatives to consider the effectiveness of out-of-school provision and to raise questions about how to conceptualise effectiveness. Secondly, it considers perspectives on exclusion from other countries, particularly the USA. Thirdly, it puts exclusion from school in the broader policy context of social exclusion and the so-called 'Third Way' of tackling social problems. This last issue is considered mainly in the concluding chapter. The intention is not to undervalue the connections between schooling on the one hand and social and economic structures and relationships on the other. Nor would we contest the needs of teachers to develop a 'meta language' to explain and describe what they do and why they do it. Nevertheless, it is of limited practical value to teachers to be continually reminded that there are severe social and economic structural constraints on their practice. Rather our approach has been to describe and explain alternatives to exclusion at the level of the day-to-day experience of teachers and pupils. This may be read as giving greater weight to the agency of individual schools than is warranted in Britain at the end of the twentieth century. Yet the examples of alternatives to exclusion come from real schools coping with the complicated and multi-faceted job of teaching. These schools are tackling exclusion in a context in which there is:

- an increase in the psychosocial problems among young people (Rutter and Smith, 1995)
- an increased rate of family breakdown through divorce and a rise in the number of single parent families
- a widening gap between the poor and others (EIS, 1998; Poverty Alliance, 1998; Mortimore and Whitty, 1999)
- a cultural response to alienating and alienated behaviour, which sees excluded pupils as culprits rather than victims (DfE, 1994; Blyth and Milner, 1994) or as having little entitlement to education (Lloyd-Smith, 1993; Abbots and Parsons, 1993)
- challenge to traditional notions of masculine and feminine identity and behaviour (Weiner *et al.*, 1997)
- a government policy to promote a quasi-market in schooling. Such

policies include parental choice of school, devolved school management, the publication of comparative school performance in league tables and targets for schools in terms of specific improvements in pupil attainments. These policies are seen as producing a general climate in which schools are reluctant to admit or maintain pupils who threaten their image or performance (Munn *et al.*, 1998; Parsons, 1999).

Although the nuances of the context vary in the different constituent parts of the United Kingdom, the context itself is sufficiently pervasive to affect the day-to-day reality of schooling across the land. The Scottish focus of the research should not detract from the potential applicability of its findings to schools in England, Wales and Northern Ireland.

Chapter 1 begins with an account of the impact of exclusion on young people and their families using their voices to convey the reality of exclusion and its effects. Chapter 2 places these accounts in terms of statistics on exclusion and raises questions about what counts as a high or low excluding school. It provides answers to these questions with examples of different ways of measuring the exclusion rates of the schools involved in the Scottish research.

Chapter 3 considers the policy context in which alternatives to exclusion operate. It describes English and Scottish legislation on exclusion and summarises the key differences between them. It highlights policy and practice dilemmas which schools face in trying to avoid excluding pupils.

Chapter 4 draws extensively on the findings of our research to highlight four key aspects of school ethos which are seen as underpinning exclusion practice. These are teacher beliefs about the purpose of teaching and who counts as an acceptable pupil; the flexibility of the curriculum on offer; schools' relations with the 'outside world'; and decision-making structures about exclusion. The chapter then outlines examples of strategies for developing a positive ethos, drawn from development work in Scotland, and concludes with a description of the Scottish Schools Ethos Network, a vehicle for encouraging school self-evaluation of ethos and promoting positive developments.

Chapter 5 describes whole-school responses to challenging behaviour. These range from sanctions and the use of internal exclusion, to the positive role which on-site units and behaviour support staff can play. Examples of in-school alternatives in action are given, using findings from our research.

Chapter 6 changes focus from whole-school level responses to responses focusing on the needs of individual pupils and their teachers. There is a discussion of the therapeutic continuum and of what non-specialist teachers can offer pupils in difficulty in terms of a therapeutic experience and counselling skills. Examples are given in this chapter of preventing exclusion through teaching pupils specific survival skills. It concludes by drawing attention to teachers' needs for support and supervision in these roles.

Out-of-school provision for children in trouble is the focus of Chapter 7. There are still considerable numbers of pupils out of mainstream school and/or in special provision for those with social, emotional and behavioural difficulties. This chapter reviews the difficulties of conceptualising and measuring the effectiveness of such provision. It also summarises the arguments for and against the existence of alternative provision.

Chapter 8 compares British policy and practice on exclusion with that of other countries with broadly similar education systems, particularly the USA. Britain has been prone to borrow policy and practices from the USA, especially in the field of special education. Comparisons are made in terms of rates of exclusion, concepts of inclusion and of characteristics of excluded pupils. A number of common themes and issues across countries are identified.

Finally, Chapter 9 considers the broader policy context of social exclusion and asks what is realistic for schools to achieve in this context.

There are two appendices. Appendix 1 summarises key features of the Scottish education system, for those English and other readers to whom it is unfamiliar; while Appendix 2 describes the Children's Hearing System, the welfare based approach to children in trouble.

The book, of course, does not provide a recipe for tackling exclusion nor a recipe for change. Schools have individual histories, traditions and contexts which make it impractical to import 'what works' in one context unproblematically to another. Neither, however, does the book suggest that every school must find its own path to reducing exclusion in an uncharted landscape. It offers a number of key contour lines for schools to use in planning their journey to provide alternatives to exclusion. These range from a critical review of the school's ethos to the use of in-school units and bases, inter-agency working, working with parents and the employment of counselling skills by teachers. The aim is to provide starting points for schools to review their policy and practice by providing real examples of a number of alternatives to exclusion in action, and placing these alternatives in a wider policy context within the UK and internationally.

Acknowledgements

Many people have contributed to the ideas and evidence contained in this book. Our sincere thanks to all those who participated in the empirical phase of the research, especially to headteachers, teachers, educational psychologists, social workers and education authority officials. All took part very willingly, sparing time to be interviewed and completing lengthy questionnaires. The work of the research team benefited greatly from the constructive advice and support of an advisory committee, chaired by Bob McKay, Director of Education, Perth and Kinross Council. The committee met regularly over the two and a half years of the project and provided help at key stages. Colleagues in the Faculty of Education encouraged us, criticised some of our ideas and generally provided a supportive environment in which to develop our thinking. Lesley Scullion typed successive drafts with her customary efficiency and good humour. Our respective husbands and children tolerated the disruption to family and social life which writing a book necessarily entails. Marianne Lagrange at Sage provided the right amount of friendly encouragement as we began to fall behind our original timetable. We appreciate her tolerance and support. We are also grateful to the Scottish Office for funding a series of research projects on indiscipline in school which has permitted us to undertake a larger scale of empirical work than would otherwise have been possible.

Finally, the book owes a great deal to the young people and their parents who had experienced exclusion and were prepared to talk about it and the impact it had on their lives. Some interviews meant the reliving of painful experiences for them as they recounted the other stresses and strains to which exclusion was added. The words of Wayne T* sum up the reasons most were willing to take part:

> Well, see when [my teacher] asked me if I wanted to do this and she said what it was about and she said it would make a difference and all that, I said, 'Aye, definitely'. If I knew it was just that nothing would be getting done about it, I wouldn't have bothered, but because it's getting all recorded, I don't mind talking.

We hope this book contributes to making a difference to exclusion policy and practice.

---

*All names of pupils, parents and schools are fictitious to protect their identity.

1

Exclusion and Excluded Pupils

The minute the child is put out of the class, you've started something. You've started their sense of, 'I'm not coping', and a lot of children, to keep their pride, will suggest it doesn't matter. 'Throw me out again, see if I care.' ... I think that for the people that are involved in dealing out exclusions, [exclusion] has become like lines. It's meaningless, absolutely meaningless. I don't think they realise just what an impact it has on the family and on the children.

(Educational psychologist, Lubnaig Secondary School)

What does it mean to be excluded from school? Exclusion is officially the most serious sanction that British schools can use, yet, as the above quotation suggests and as many surveys have shown, it is something that thousands of school pupils experience, some of them more than once. What sort of impact does it have on pupils and on their families? This chapter reports the experience of exclusion from the point of view of pupils and their parents. The focus is on eleven pupils who experienced exclusion and on its consequences both for them and for their families.

It begins by reporting pupils' feelings about exclusion and describes these in terms of initial reactions, during time out of school and on return to school. Very few pupils seemed aware of the potentially negative effects of exclusion on employment prospects or on life chances more generally. The chapter then describes the effects of exclusion on family life, highlighting the many stresses and strains which these families were experiencing. It concludes by summarising the alternatives to exclusion which these pupils and their families believed would be effective.

Pupils' experience of exclusion

The eleven pupils interviewed as part of the exclusions research project (Cullen *et al.*, 1996) experienced exclusion from school in a range of ways. Their experience depended on their age, their own and others' views about gender appropriate behaviour, their own view of the seriousness of their behaviour, their view of school in general and the circumstances of their home life. In many ways, their views and circumstances were similar to those of other excluded young people and their families (see e.g. Cohen *et al.*, 1994; Cullingford & Morrison, 1996; de Pear and Garner, 1996; John, 1996; Hayden, 1997; Kinder *et al.*, 1997; Brodie, 1998; Kinder *et al.*, 1999). The studies report feelings of rejection, unfairness and of being labelled a troublemaker on the part of excluded pupils. They also report stress, strain and feelings of helplessness on the part of families who are often trying to cope with a number of disadvantages including poverty, ill-health and inadequate housing. The studies are necessarily small-scale as in-depth interviewing is expensive and so they do not provide a robust statistical basis from which to generalise about the effects of exclusion on young people and their families. Nevertheless, listening to the views of children and parents is important in itself and, cumulatively, small-scale studies of the views of pupils and their parents 'can be used in a dynamic way, helping to illustrate the shortcomings of schools in particular and society as a whole. This may, of course, be one reason why we do not wish to listen to them' (de Pear and Garner, 1996: 154/155).

How the pupils felt about exclusion

The eight boys and three girls interviewed ranged in age from 7–8-year-olds to 16–17-year-olds. They were all perceived by their schools as difficult pupils: ten of them had been excluded more than once and they all had a history of being in trouble in school – some also had been in trouble with the police. They were perceived by their schools as being at the extreme end of behaviour problems in their respective schools. Several of them had been threatened with removal from the school register (permanent exclusion). They all experienced exclusion, first and foremost, as a strong, negative emotional reaction. They felt:

- rejected (not wanted, kicked out, chucked out)
- angry ('I wanted to hit him')
- hard done by (unfair, surprised)
- worried (about parents' reactions)
- upset

- scared
- shocked.

The last resort punishment had been used against them: their negative feelings are not surprising. Yet they displayed a strong sense of justice in reflecting on their own exclusions. Most of the pupils interviewed differentiated between what they regarded as serious offences that deserved the ultimate sanction and those that they regarded as trivial for which exclusion was inappropriate. Jean A. put it like this:

> If they're going to chuck me out for something I deserve to get chucked out for, then fair enough. I didn't think I deserved to get chucked out because I didn't do a punishment exercise. It's different if you have been fighting or if you've been causing trouble in the class.
>
> (Jean A., Coruisk Secondary School)

The pupils accepted that violence against teachers or against other pupils was unacceptable and usually deserved exclusion. Thus, for example, Brian B. accepted that he was justly excluded for having been involved in an incident where a pupil's hair had been set alight, albeit by accident. However, some of them made the point that there may be a difference between violence, fighting or other strongly anti-social behaviour that is 'meant' and that which is not 'meant' to be serious. In the latter case, such as fighting between friends, some of the pupils thought exclusion was inappropriate because the situation could be resolved by using less serious strategies. Indeed, Jean A. recounted how a fight she had been involved in was resolved by teachers. They listened to both sides of the story, made the offenders sit outside the head's office for two lessons and then sat down with the girls, talking it all through, warning that a repeat of the fighting would result in exclusion. Her reaction was to decide to behave and to make friends with the girl: 'now we're the best of pals'.

Feeling a sense of injustice

Sometimes pupils expressed a sense of injustice because they felt that their side of the story of the incident that had led directly to exclusion had never been heard. The pupils felt particularly aggrieved when they thought they had been 'picked on', singled out for serious punishment that was not meted out to others. Michael N., for example, was excluded for swearing at a teacher but, in his account, he had sworn at girls who were squirting mousse down his back and the teachers just happened to be there and to have heard him. His sense of injustice that 'they said [the swearing] was deliberate but it wasn't' was exacerbated by his belief that, '[other] folk get off with swearing all the time'. As he explained:

> In the class, just after I got back from the exclusion, there was a lassie swearing and the teacher didnae bother but when I got caught, I got chucked out.
>
> (Michael N., Lubnaig Secondary School)

Five other pupils also spoke about feeling singled out by teachers because of having a reputation for bad behaviour. Their sense of injustice was greatest when this reputation was gained not personally but by proxy – for example, on account of the behaviour of their older siblings. Two pupils, James C. from Coruisk Secondary School and Robbie M. from Tummel Secondary School, had even changed schools previously because of encountering teachers' hostility as a result of their older siblings' behaviour. James had experienced this in Primary 1 and moved school; Robbie in first year of his previous secondary:

> When I went to the school, I was down at the office for something and the [headteacher] asked me my name. She was just talking to me and I telt her my name and that's when the problems started because my name was [—], because I had something to do with [names his older cousin and older brothers].
>
> (Robbie M., Tummel Secondary School)

A bad reputation by proxy could also occur because of living in the 'wrong' part of town. Interestingly, the two cases recounted to us involved pupils who came from disadvantaged areas of towns but, through parental choice, attended schools with good reputations in the 'leafy suburbs'. Theresa W., from Ness Secondary School, believed that some of the teachers treated her and other pupils from the 'wrong' part of town differently – for example, she believed that her English teacher marked her down and that she got into trouble more than similar pupils from the 'right' part of town:

TW:	Sometimes [the teachers] pick on you and certain ones pick on you because of where you come from. Like, in first year, I had this English teacher and he didn't really like me and he was giving me grade 3s and 4s. When I went into second year, I was getting grade 1s and 2s because I had a better teacher.
Interviewer:	When you say they pick on you because of where you are from, what do you mean?

| TW: | They just treat you differently from people from [this] area sometimes – only some of them, other [teachers] are OK. |

A little later:

| Interviewer: | When you say, treated differently . . . |
| TW: | Just little things like that you would get into trouble more than another person. |

(Theresa W., Ness Secondary School)

Mark L. from Fyne Secondary School also believed that he got into trouble more because of where he was from and challenged the interviewer to 'ask anyone from [his area] that's in the school and they'll say exactly the same'. He told the interviewer that his sister, too, had encountered this prejudice from the senior manager (since retired) who excluded her and called her, 'just another scum from [area of town]'.

Some teachers seen as inconsistent

Sometimes, also, the pupils felt that the system was unfair because teachers in the school did not behave consistently. The pupils were aware that what happened as a result of an infringement of rules could be a bit of a lottery, depending on which teacher was involved and even on the mood a teacher happened to be in on the day. For example, pupils reported that some teachers always referred incidents, such as failure to complete a punishment exercise, up to the head of department who would then refer it to the headteacher, making exclusion a likely outcome where another teacher might simply give another deadline for completion. Equally, in a good mood, a teacher might ignore the use of low-voiced swearing but, in a bad mood, might refer a similar incident to the head as verbal abuse.

As well as not liking inconsistency, the pupils greatly disliked teachers who shouted. This was a particular problem for the boys interviewed who seemed to become fired up by teachers shouting at them. For Michael N. it was especially difficult to cope with, as shouting by a male authority figure triggered memories of years of violence and abuse by his father from whom the family had fled. Michael's angry reaction got him into trouble time and again – even though he understood why shouting made him angry, he had not yet managed to break the patterned response. Michael was striving to overcome his anger, though, with the support of an educational psychologist, a social worker and a therapist. (Ironically, during our interview with Michael, the teacher who shouted at him most could be heard yelling abuse at another child in the corridor outside.)

The pupils were consistent in describing 'bad' teachers as those who shouted and threatened; 'good' teachers, on the other hand, were those who were more relaxed in interpersonal relations, who listened to pupils and talked to them and who took time to explain the work. Good teachers were also sometimes described as 'strict', but only in relation to insisting that pupils were at school to work – not strict in terms of adhering to the letter of the disciplinary system. Indeed, pupils appreciated and appeared to have responded well to being offered 'second chances' by individual classroom teachers. Of course, there is a balance to be struck between flexibility and consistency in matters of discipline but true fairness requires such a balance. It was noteworthy that five of the pupils interviewed spoke about how they had enjoyed primary school much better than secondary because of the better relationship they had had with their teachers there – in primary school, they would have had only one main class teacher per school year.

What happened at home

After being in trouble at school, excluded pupils then faced being in serious trouble at home. It is noteworthy that even the parents whom the school perceived as unsupportive of the school were regarded by the excluded pupils as angry and upset with them because of the exclusion. Two of the boys were hit by their fathers and another boy was frightened that his mother would hit him. On first being excluded, one girl ran away rather than face going home and one boy thought seriously about running away. Another boy, James C., described how he pushed the letter notifying his parents of his exclusion through the letterbox and ran away because he feared his father's anger. (This fear was likely to have been justified – at the time of the research, social workers no longer visited families in that street because of the reputation for violence that James' father had.) Most of the parents felt they had to punish their child further. These further punishments included:

- hitting
- shouting
- exclusion from family life for a while (keeping the young people in their room alone for a day or days, or refusing to let them in to the house all day)

- exclusion from socialising with friends
- stopping pocket money for a time.

It was clear that the pupils interviewed did not like the experience of being excluded, nor their parents' reactions when they got home. In addition, the combined effect of the school exclusion and the parental punishments resulted in the time away from school being experienced largely as sedentary boredom, as a time of 'sitting aboot the hoose a' day'. Some of those on short exclusions saw it as 'a wee holiday' or as 'just three days off' or as an opportunity to help their mother with the housework, but others were so bored they realised that being at school was preferable. Only one of the pupils was given work to do by the school. Two of the oldest pupils used their own initiative and took the opportunity to do homework or some extra work.

The loss of education incurred obviously depended on the length of exclusion. One boy was out of school for months before eventually, through social work intervention, being given a part-time place in an off-site unit and was then gradually re-integrated back into his school. For him, the time lost was seriously damaging to his achievement at school. But even for those out on short exclusions, if they were already having problems with reading and writing, catching up on return to school was not easy. Three of the pupils had so much difficulty with writing (sometimes they expressed this as finding it 'boring') that they refused to do punishment exercises (lines) and as a result were excluded. To them, being excluded was preferable to being made to write out punishment exercises. For these pupils, catching up on even three to five days' work on return to school was a nightmare. Four of the pupils did not see catching up as a problem but these were pupils who quite liked school and were doing reasonably well academically. For example, Isobel K., aged 15, was excluded for five weeks for stealing but worked away on her own at home during that time and did not have any problems catching up when she went back to school. She was studying for eight Standard Grades and expected to stay on for fifth and sixth year and to go to university.

Coping with returning to school

Returning to school after an exclusion was hard not only because of catching up on missed work but also because of the reactions of peers. Isobel K. spoke about being called a 'thief' and being asked in a hostile manner, 'why have you come back?' Others felt pressure from their friends to continue behaving badly even when, as a result of the exclusion, they had themselves resolved to change. Hence Theresa W. was again excluded – this time for smoking which she had done because she was 'just trying to go along with all my friends'. Michael N. was making a valiant attempt to behave in school but felt undermined by his previous friends who called him a 'sook' [i.e. sucking up to teachers]:

> If you're good and sit down and get on with your work and that, they [his pals] say you're a big sook and all this, but if you get excluded they dinnae really bother [i.e. care].
>
> (Michael N., Lubnaig Secondary School)

His reaction was to avoid these boys at breaktime and to involve himself in playing football rather than following them into trouble. But another boy spoke about his friends' concerns for him, expressed on his return to school:

> They'd say, 'Oh no, Wayne, you'll get into deep trouble' and things like that. They'd say that I shouldn't have done it and stuff like that.
>
> (Wayne T., Ness School)

One pupil was aware that having been excluded had changed his reputation in the community. Other mothers told their children not to go round with him because he'd been 'kicked out of school'. Only a small number of the pupils understood that a history of exclusion from school might have longer-term negative consequences when, for example, they tried to get a job:

> When I'm getting a job, people will look at my records and things like that and they might not employ me because I've been suspended. . . . They think you could swear at an employee or something like that or could end up hitting them or swear at a customer or something like that. 'He can't control his temper.'
>
> (Wayne T., age 14, Ness Secondary School)

Table 1.1 summarises the different stages at which exclusion affects the pupils concerned.

The effects of exclusion on family life

Exclusion is not only a way of punishing a pupil, it also punishes the parents in a sense because they are responsible for their son or daughter during the exclusion. This can be awkward for working parents or parents with other commitments during the day. In recognition of

Table 1.1. The staged effects of exclusion on pupils

Stage 1 immediate	Stage 2 initial reaction at home	Stage 3 during time out of school	Stage 4 on return to school	Stage 5 long term
• strong negative feelings of e.g. rejection, fear, injustice	• angry reaction from parents • further punish-ments from parents	• boredom (which sometimes made school seem better) • missing out on school work • missing out on time with school friends • negative reputation in the community	• negative reaction of peers • negative reputation among teachers • difficulties catching up with school work	• fear that it would negatively affect job prospects

this, some schools were willing to bend the rules to prevent parents perceived as supportive from being put under further pressure by the exclusion of their son or daughter. This was the case for three of the pupils we interviewed.

One of these pupils was Matthew P. (age 7) who had a long history of serious behaviour problems that had proved intractable in the face of a whole range of interventions. He had been formally excluded, had had behaviour cards, a behaviour programme based on praise, his bad behaviour ignored, classroom assistants working with him, a volunteer from a local family resource centre taking him out during his leisure time, an educational psychologist working with him – none of these interventions had changed his behaviour in school (at least in part, according to his mother, because she couldn't always manage to be consistent about behaviour at home). In the term following our interview with him Matthew was to begin attending a special school – the hope was that being in a class of six, where he would get the attention he so deeply craved, would make a difference. His mother worked every morning. At first, when Matthew was excluded, she had been very angry with the school but gradually she had realised that the school was trying to help her and her son. She reached an agreement with the school that if Matthew misbehaved during the morning, the school would look after him until she got in from work and then she would come and take him home for the rest of the day. Although this arrangement was supportive in that it meant she didn't have to take time off her work, it did mean that she was worn down. She had to deal with Matthew's difficult behaviour during the time he was at home normally, and all the times he was sent home when he should have been at school. She felt she had no one to turn to to share the stress of coping with her son.

In an attempt to support her parents, Isobel K. (age 15) was temporarily, rather than permanently, excluded. Like Matthew, she had had a long history of serious behaviour problems (all relating to theft and fraud) that had proved intractable in the face of a whole range of interventions. She had been repeatedly excluded, had social workers working with her, she had been before the Children's Panel. At the time we interviewed her she was under a supervision order, she had a carer who took her out on leisure activities three afternoons a week, she had seen an educational psychologist and the police had been involved. Again, none of these interventions had changed Isobel's behaviour for very long although her mother was hopeful that recent improvements would be more permanent. The temporary exclusions were helpful in the mother's view because they allowed her to keep her daughter away from school, and therefore out of temptation's way, legally – otherwise, the mother would have had to keep her daughter off school and risk getting into trouble for that. Mrs K. was, however, grateful that the school had not 'kicked [Isobel] out and kept her out'. She was convinced that gender played a part in the school's attitude, believing that, if a boy had done what her daughter had done, that boy would have been removed from the school register.

The third pupil who was treated more leniently in an attempt to help the parents was Jean A. (age 15), who had a long history of serious attendance problems that had, again, proved intractable in the face of a range of punitive measures: parental punishments, police involvement, and being taken into care temporarily. When we interviewed her, Jean was in her final term at school – she was to leave at the end of the autumn term after her 16th birthday. Rather than being excluded again for her poor attendance without good reason, she was being educated within the Support Unit of her mainstream school where she was making progress. Her mother recognised that while the school dealt with her daughter as a discipline problem, both she and her daughter had found it difficult to relate to teachers who, they felt, put the school rather than the pupils first. Once her daughter was 'taken under the wing' of the Support Unit teacher, though, she acknowledged that the school 'really, really looked after her'.

Understanding the parents' position

One of the key issues that these three examples illustrate is that while schools have to deal with the problems of a number of pupils during school hours, parents have to deal with the problems of their child or children during all the out-of-school hours. At the end of the school day, teachers can go home: parents of an excluded child have no reprieve. At least these three parents felt that the schools were acknowledging the problems exclusion caused for them and that exclusion was no solution to the problems of their child. Indeed, substantial investment had been made in trying to support the children at school. Other parents we interviewed had not been treated with such understanding.

The main effects of exclusion on these other families are summarised in Table 1.2 (page 12). Although irritation and inconvenience may not seem terribly important effects of exclusion on family life, when it is remembered that some of these families were already under a great deal of stress through, for example, divorce proceedings, recent remarriage and the birth of a new baby, maternal and sibling ill-health, other siblings being 'looked after' by the local authority, further stress caused by exclusion only exacerbated difficulties. As Table 1.2 shows, too, it also caused further problems within families by leading to arguments.

Most of the parents we interviewed were supportive of the school and also accepted that exclusion was necessary when something serious had happened. Like the pupils, they made a distinction between serious offences where exclusion was justified and exclusion for 'silly things' but some also understood the argument that seemingly trivial incidents in themselves may have a cumulative effect, resulting in serious disruption to the work of the class:

> It's all backchat. It's being the class clown generally – which means he is just really disrupting the whole class from their work. That is the point the school is making, which I agree with.
>
> (Mrs M.)

Although, then, parents interviewed accepted exclusion as a punishment, they did seem to be vexed by three aspects: i) problems over exclusion procedures, ii) the loss of education incurred and iii) the ineffectiveness of exclusion in changing the child's behaviour.

Parents were particularly cross about exclusion procedures that

Table 1.2.   Effects of exclusion on families: the views of parents

irritation with the child	'He gets on my nerves.' (Mrs. B) 'He's got a 10 day suspension [i.e. exclusion]. He's got two weeks off school – to do what? To get under my feet.' (Mrs M.)
inconvenience	'You cannae get your [house]work done the same.' (Mrs B.) 'I've got to watch [look after] him.' (Mr C.) 'There was a lot of inconvenience for me as well. I couldn't go out anywhere . . .' (Mr R.)
stress caused by frustration with the system	'You feel as if you could scream.'; 'I was in a real bad temper with what was happening'; 'I was really mad at that, you know'; 'You feel as if you are banging your head against a brick wall, this is it.' (Mrs M.)
family arguments	Robbie M.'s exclusion caused arguments with his siblings; arguments between his mother and his father (who were separated); arguments between his father and his stepmother (who had a new baby). Mark L.'s exclusion caused arguments between his mother and father: 'I take the money out of his pocket and keep him indoors. That drives him off his head. That drives the wife up the wall and all!' (Mr L.)
mother stigmatised	'I said, "It's not me who is the problem". [The headteacher] was wanting somebody to start coming about my house, a social worker, looking into your background and that sort of thing. . . . It ended up with a big fight because she said to my [ex]husband, "Do you think your wife is not coping?" . . . I said, "I'm left with all the hassle I've had with my husband, I'm left with four kids and all the rest of it – keep a house, do this, do that, ill-health – and you are telling me you're putting in a social worker! No way! If anybody comes near this door, there will be hell to pay." ' (Mrs. M.)
siblings stigmatised	'[Michael N.'s sister] is a different kettle of fish. She's very brainy and the teachers at school get on to her about [Michael N.]. . . . She just says that it's got nothing to do with her but she gets embarrassed.' (Mrs N.) '[Robbie's brother] walked up the wrong side of the stair and she [teacher] said to him, "Why are you walking up there, Mister [M.]? Are you trying to come [Robbie's] patter? [i.e. copy Robbie's behaviour]". She was trying to pick on him for things.' (Mrs M.)

served to increase the use of exclusion. Sometimes these were education authority procedures; sometimes they were school procedures. Examples cited included:

- three referrals for bad behaviour automatically leading to exclusion – even if each incident had been in itself trivial. Parents, like the pupils, spoke about failure to complete a punishment exercise being one such incident that could quickly escalate into exclusion.
- each exclusion automatically being for a longer length of time, regardless of the relative seriousness of the incident.
- the necessity of a parent visiting the school to speak to the headteacher before a pupil could be reintegrated. Parents in difficult circumstances, such as ill-health or having a new baby, would have liked to be allowed to discuss things over the phone. Refusal to allow this, in two cases, led to the exclusion period being extended, in one case for an extra week.
- the necessity to involve an external professional before a pupil was readmitted. In one case, after a meeting was cancelled at short notice by the external professional, the child remained excluded for a further month until another meeting could be arranged.

Most of the parents interviewed spoke about their concern over the loss of education that exclusion involved (only one of the case study pupils was given school work to do during the exclusion period). Mrs B, whose son, Brian, was out of school for months, was concerned that he was 'bound to have lost a lot of education'. She found it hard to understand the apparent lack of priority given to reintegration by senior education officials:

> You'd think that with them being excluded that the head one, well, whoever it is, would want the bairns [i.e. children] to get back into school as quick as possible. I think they should try something for to get them back into school quicker than what it takes.
>
> (Mrs B., parent, Coruisk Secondary School)

Other parents, too, spoke of their son or daughter 'missing out' or 'missing out a lot' on education. As the quotations below illustrate, they were annoyed that school work was not sent home to be done during the exclusion. Without school work, exclusion was just 'a wee holiday' and, in addition, catching up on missed work added to the problems of returning to school afterwards.

> I feel angry about it. . . . They don't even send work home so he misses out again. So if he gets excluded for a week, he's misses a

week's work, plus another week until I can come up to the school [for the reintegration meeting] so he's missing out a lot.

(Mrs N., parent, Lubnaig Secondary School)

Sending them home with no work, nothing to do, have a wee holiday, come back and fall back into place with the classes just is not the answer because obviously he is missing two weeks of work in each class.

(Mrs M., parent, Tummel Secondary School)

Mark L. was in the year when Standard Grade examinations are taken when we interviewed him and his father about his exclusion experiences. His father was very worried about the loss of education Mark was incurring through exclusion, especially since he had already lost a lot of schooling due to ill-health:

As he got a bit older, he got asthma bad so he was behind in a lot of his schooling. . . . I thought myself that he was doing not bad and catching up with his work, but I think these suspensions [i.e. exclusions] retards him a wee bit and all, you know. Because you feel as if he's catching up in work, and if he's suspended maybe for two, maybe for three weeks – if it's something the teacher has got to sort and maybe involving him and another boy [or] maybe two or three boys, by the time you get to the bottom of this and things are sorted out and he goes back, well, that's him three weeks behind again. And he's at an important time, now, education-wise.

(Mr L., parent, Fyne Secondary School)

The lack of evidence that exclusion had any ameliorating effect on behaviour also troubled parents. Their experience was of the so-called 'last resort' punishment being resorted to over and over again to little or no effect. Some of the parents had ideas about what might work better in terms of changing behaviour. These were linked to their understandings of why their son or daughter behaved badly in school.

Changing behaviour without using exclusion

Table 1.3 provides a sample of parents' (and pupils') understandings of the reasons behind the behaviour that led to exclusion, and of punishments and supportive strategies that were, or might have been, more effective in changing such behaviour for the better. Similar tables could be constructed for all the pupils in the study.

A number of themes emerge strongly from pupils' and parents' views about behaviour. First, most of the pupils and parents gave more than one underlying reason for the behaviour, indicating the often complex interplay of pressures that can come together to create a disciplinary incident in school. A second theme is that most thought some kind of alternative punishment that kept the pupil in school and busy would be more of a deterrent than exclusion. This suggests that exclusion loses its effect when it is used in response to apparently trivial matters and/or when it is equated with holidays from school. The importance of positive teacher–pupil relationships, that is, ones that are respectful, relaxed and engaged, also comes across clearly. From pupil and parent accounts, it would appear that just as pupils lose their temper inappropriately, so can teachers – the difference is that pupils, too often, seem to be expected to accept such lack of control from the adults around them. Consistency in the standards of behaviour expected among teachers in different classes and between home and school – establishing a sense of fairness – is a fourth key theme. Finally, the agency of the pupils in deciding to change their own behaviour emerges strongly. The decision to change behaviour was prompted by a desire to please parents and/or a recognition that school could offer positive experiences if approached with a different attitude. Each of these themes, and many other points made by the pupils and parents, are discussed further throughout this book.

This chapter has focused on the personal experiences of exclusion of a small number of young people and their families. It is an attempt to go beyond statistics to convey something of the flavour of the stresses and strains which were part of the everyday lives of young people and their families. Exclusion from school added to these. Many of the schools which these young people attended were helpful and supportive to them and their families. They provided specialist help, were flexible in timetabling and provided space for young people to reflect on their behaviour and its consequences. Other schools appear from these accounts, and from research, to have been less willing to understand the background to troubled behaviour or to support in-school strategies to help change it. Chapter 4 explores the idea of school ethos as an explanation for these differences among schools and suggests ways in which schools can evaluate their ethos and develop more positive approaches to young people in trouble. First, however, we consider how widespread exclusion is and how many young people and their families may be experiencing the effects described in this chapter.

Table 1.3. Changing behaviour without using exclusion from school: views of some case study pupils and parents

views of pupils and parents	reason/s behind behaviour	more effective alternatives to exclusion from school		other change mechanisms
		alternative punishment/s	supportive alternative	
Mathew P. (age 7)	• the teacher 'makes me angry. He makes me shout at him.' • the classroom work is too hard • 'I cannae behave myself' because other children would not let him join in at break • feeling 'sad and angry'	• lines • a detention	• a better relationship with the teacher • being allowed to play with a toy at breaktimes	
Mrs P.	• Matthew hates school and hates his teacher • does not like authority • does not accept responsibility for his own behaviour • egocentric 'he thinks about nothing but himself and he's very selfish' • inconsistency at home • a few personal problems, a bit of jealousy of his younger brother • 'just the way he is'		• one-to-one attention • more choice about what to do	
Michael N. (age 13)	• anger (at having mousse squirted on him) • anger (at teacher shouting at him unfairly) • root of anger is violent abuse of his mother (by his dad) and sexual abuse of his sister (by his step dad) • sense of injustice – that teachers didn't like him and picked on him • sense of injustice – other pupils teased him for living in a women's refuge (with his mother and sister)	• detention – in the in-school support centre with work to do	• teachers who talk to you rather than shout at you • anger management • relaxation therapy • to move away from area (i.e. a fresh start)	• own decision to 'be good in class' • building better relationships with teachers • decided to do this to save his mother 'a lot of hassle' • own decision to work hard and to avoid trouble at breaktime by e.g. playing football with new friends

Mrs N.	• interaction with one or two other boys (i.e. influence of peers) • hunger (went out with no breakfast) • personality clashes with some teachers • Michael feels his reputation means some teachers pick on him • Michael's mood • mental abuse suffered at hands of his father left Michael with a lot of anger • trouble coping with a male authority figure • finds some subjects boring and won't do the work (e.g. maths)	• internal exclusion in support centre with work to do	• that grouping of boys to be put in separate classes • ensure he eats breakfast • letting all his teachers know that he does behave well in some classes and in the support centre • allow him to work on his own in support centre to 'cool off' sessions with the psychologist • praise where praise is due • consistency between home and school about behaviour (helped by use of conduct sheet to be signed by mother each night)	• Michael to keep away from boys that encourage him to misbehave – sit away from them and get on with his work
Jean A. (age 15)	• dislikes writing • short tempered (especially in the playground) – others 'call you names and nag you' • pressure to do exams	• belt (over quickly, no writing involved as with punishment exercises) • short internal exclusion (e.g. two classes)	• second chance • teachers listening to both sides of a story; discussing incident after 'cooling off' time • smaller, friendlier schools	• own decision to stay away from troublemakers
Mrs A.	• boyfriend trouble (being stalked and harassed by mentally ill ex-boyfriend) • ill-health (epilepsy) • problems relating to house tutor		• allowed to come in late to avoid ex-boyfriend • internal support unit (good relationships) • constructive leisure activities	

2

How Widespread is Exclusion?

This chapter widens the focus of Chapter 1 to consider how many pupils share the experience of exclusion. Evidence from a range of surveys in Britain is presented highlighting the likely underestimation of numbers of pupils excluded reported in official statistics. The second part of the chapter concentrates on our research and describes the patterns of exclusion in the sample of schools. It sets out some of the school characteristics, that is aspects unrelated to the individual pupil, that tend to predict whether a school will make a high or low use of exclusion.

The extent of exclusion

It is difficult to obtain accurate figures on the extent of exclusion from schools in the UK. There are several reasons for this. Firstly we know from a number of studies that informal exclusion, not officially recorded, takes place across the country (Lawrence and Hayden, 1997; Cullen et al., 1996; Parsons, 1996a, 1999; Imich, 1994; Stirling, 1992). Secondly, different legislative positions in England and Scotland mean that direct comparisons of exclusion are suspect. (Some local councils in Scotland have a policy of no permanent exclusions and there is no national fixed term period for exclusion in Scotland. Chapter 3 provides details.) Thirdly, there is wide variation in the kinds of statistics which local authorities collect. Local authorities have to rely on information supplied by schools. Parsons (1999) contends that since exclusions are becoming a performance indicator for schools there are incentives for schools to under-record if they want to show themselves in the best light they can, and this was also evident from our research (Munn et al., 1997).

As far as England is concerned, it is estimated that about 13,500 permanent exclusions had taken place in 1996/97. Parsons estimates that 10,890 pupils were permanently excluded from secondary schools, 1,856 from primary schools and 707 from special schools. The absolute numbers were worrying in themselves, but of greater concern is that numbers have grown. There was a 45 per cent increase between 1993–94 and 1995–96 in primary schools and an 18 per cent increase over the same period in secondary schools (Parsons, 1996; Lawrence and Hayden, 1997). Fixed term exclusions are about eight times more numerous than permanent exclusions (Parsons, 1999).

The characteristics of excluded pupils

An analysis of the characteristics of excluded pupils shows that boys are around four times as likely to be excluded as girls and African-Caribbean pupils are excluded between three and six times more often than their white peers (Parsons, 1999; Commission for Racial Equality, 1996; Stirling, 1993; Brodie and Berridge, undated). Smaller-scale studies show the rise in numbers of pupils being excluded from a special school in one local authority (Stirling, 1992, 1994) and the likelihood of children from single parent or 'reconstituted' families being excluded in greater proportions than their peers in 'normal' two parent families in a particular school (Ashford, 1994). For both fixed term and permanent exclusions the rates increase with age to peak at 14/15-year-olds.

Patterns of exclusion vary in terms of type of local authority. London boroughs excluded a greater proportion of children than either counties or metropolitan areas. Inner London boroughs have double the rates for metropolitan authorities and counties (Parsons, 1996, 1999). Parsons also suggests that the permanent exclusion rate for Inner London authorities at secondary level is equivalent to one in every 130 pupils.

No equivalent statistics exist for Scotland although a national picture will emerge in the near future as a result of Scottish Office guidance to schools and local authorities about the kind of information about exclusion being sought (Scottish Office, 1998). A survey of 116 secondary schools and 60 primary schools provided information on pupils excluded over a specific eight month period. The information provides a snapshot of exclusions at a particular period of time and cannot be generalised to all schools in Scotland. Nevertheless, some interesting similarities with exclusion in England emerged, the most notable being that boys were up to four times more likely to be excluded than girls and rates increase with age. In primary schools the peak stage was 9/10-year-olds and in secondary school 14/15-year-olds and 15/16-year-olds. The statistics in Tables 2.1 and 2.2 report *all* exclusions of however short a nature. In general terms, between August 1994 – March 1995, 202 pupils had been excluded from 39 primary schools and 3,562 pupils had been excluded from 110 secondary schools. A further 969 pupils had been informally excluded. Thus a total of 4,740 pupils had been excluded over this period. Exclusion most commonly happened once and lasted for three days or less although about 30 per cent of pupils were excluded for longer. Detailed information on 2,619 excluded pupils was provided by schools using a specifically designed report form and this is the basis of the tables below.

Table 2.1 shows the number of times pupils had been excluded.

Table 2.2 shows the number of school days lost through exclusion.

Taken together these tables show that most pupils are excluded for a relatively short time in what might be interpreted as a short, sharp shock approach. However, 1,068 secondary pupils and 57 primary pupils lost over a week of schooling, raising questions about the existence of reintegration strategies to help pupils catch up with the work they have missed. As chapter 1 made clear, pupils see such catching up as a problem. This in turn can lead to loss of motivation and so to disaffected behaviour particularly for those who have learning difficulties.

Figure 2.1 reports the reasons given for exclusion. The reasons stated can reflect no more than the legislative grounds for exclusion and/or the space available on the form which the headteachers were asked to complete. Some of the reasons given are striking for their seeming triviality given the emphasis on exclusion as a last resort to troublesome behaviour reported by the overwhelming majority of

Table 2.1. Number of times each pupil had been excluded August 1994 – March 1995

Times excluded	Primary school pupils N = 184		Secondary school pupils N = 2,435	
	No. of pupils	%	No. of pupils	%
Once	117	64	1,699	69
Twice	34	18	455	18
3 times	15	8	191	8
4 times	14	8	68	3
5 times	2	1	37	1
Over 5 times	2	1	30	1

*Details on some pupils were missing and so totals in the tables may vary.

Table 2.2. Days lost through exclusion per pupil, August 1994 – March 1995

Times excluded	Primary school pupils N = 182		Secondary school pupils N = 2,491	
	No. of pupils	%	No. of pupils	%
One day	13	7	108	4
2 days	29	16	202	8
3 days	50	27	613	25
4 days	10	5	205	8
5 days/a week	23	13	295	12
6 days to 2 weeks	26	14	526	21
11 days to 3 weeks	12	6	183	7
16 days to 6 weeks	14	8	218	9
More than 6 weeks	5	3	141	6

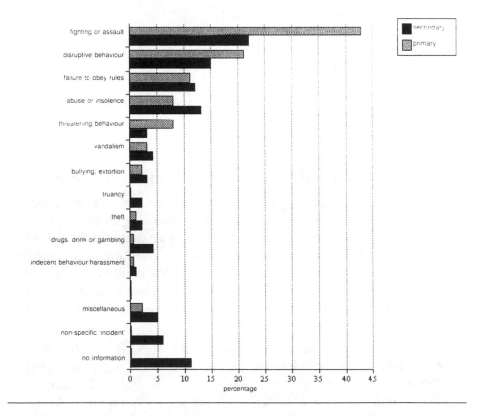

Figure 2.1. Reasons for exclusion

headteachers (data not shown). Nevertheless, a seemingly minor offence can be the straw that breaks the camel's back in a history of disaffected behaviour, a situation also reported by Normington and Kyriacou (1994). The numbers of pupils excluded for serious offences were small: using or selling drugs – 45; assault on staff – 26; carrying an offensive weapon – 19. The most common reason for both boys and girls for exclusion from both primary and secondary school was fighting (i.e. pupils fighting with each other) mostly in the playground. Chapter 4 draws attention to strategies used to train playground supervisors to promote positive behaviour. Similarly the involvement of pupils in decision making about rules, rewards and sanctions, and the use of praise to recognise positive behaviour are strategies which can reduce offences such as disruptive behaviour and failure to obey rules, common reasons for exclusion.

The full report of the research project is available from:

Pamela Munn
Professor of Curriculum Research
Associate Dean (Postgraduate) and Director of the Graduate School Faculty of Education
Holyrood Road
Edinburgh EH8 8AQ.
Tel: 0131 651 6175
Fax: 0131 558 6678
email: pamela.munn@ed.ac.uk

Characteristics of high and low excluding schools

We know from the growing body of research on school effectiveness (see Sammons *et al.*, 1997 for a review) that schools with similar kinds of pupils vary in the boost they give to pupil attainments. This body of research defines effectiveness in terms of attainments in public examination results and lists of characteristics of effective schools have emerged. In such lists the importance of a clear and consistently applied behaviour policy usually feature. For example, Sammons *et al.* (1997:172–173) report that:

> the benefits of a clear and consistently applied whole school approach to student behaviour and discipline and high staff expectations for student behaviour were evident in the explanations of better than predicted total GCSE and English performance. In contrast, significant behaviour problems and an inconsistent approach were related to poorer than predicted mathematics results.

In order to achieve positive student behaviour it is evident that staff at all levels need to share a common vision/goals and accept the need for consistency of approach.

We know very little about the characteristics of high and low excluding schools and whether schools with similar pupil populations vary in the use they make of exclusion. Furthermore there has been very little discussion in the literature about how to measure exclusion. Most researchers have concentrated, for understandable reasons, on permanent exclusion and have tended to ignore fixed term exclusion and the variation, if any, in schools' use of this sanction. This section explores these matters. It begins by discussing how to measure exclusion before describing the characteristics of high and low excluding schools.

What counts as a high or low excluding school is not straightforward. As we shall see, this can be defined in rather different ways. The exclusion rate can relate to the number of *pupils* excluded, the number of *exclusions*, the *loss of school days* or to a combination of these. In our research six main ways were identified. These were expressed in terms of percentage of the school roll:

- excluded once
- excluded more than once
- excluded for three or fewer days
- excluded for four –10 days
- excluded for 11–20 days
- excluded for over 21 days.

Looked at school by school, the variation pattern of use of these exclusion variables was striking. The overall impression was of schools responding in idiosyncratic ways to individual pupils showing behavioural problems. Far more schools used mixtures of single and repeat exclusions, for example, than used only one or the other. Equally, far more schools had excluded pupils who had lost a number of school days falling into two, three or four of the 'days lost' variables than into only one. This is an important finding in itself because existing literature on exclusion barely touches on the complexity of the variations in how exclusion is used from school to school. It was also clear, however, that there were some patterns to be found which were shared by groups of schools. In order to detect such patterns we focused on the schools which fell within the highest and lowest 10 per cent of the range of use of each variable. This was because the ranges were so wide. For example, looking at the percentage of school roll excluded more than once the range was 0.11 per cent to 10.54 per cent of roll. Such a wide range meant that it would be unwise to attempt to apply any sophisticated statistical modelling techniques with a view to establishing school effects.

High excluding schools

No school fell within the highest 10 per cent for all six variables as Table 2.3 shows.

Therefore, we decided to look in more detail at schools which could be thought of as high excluders for different reasons, namely, that they fell in the top 10 per cent of schools in the sample for their use of:

- single exclusions *and* repeat exclusions
- repeat exclusions more often than single exclusions
- exclusions totalling 21 or more days per pupil (during the time covered by the report form)
- four or more of the variables.

Table 2.3. Patterns of high exclusion within and across six variables

		Times excluded			Loss of school days		
Schools falling in highest 10% of users EA	School	single exclusions per pupil	repeat exclusions per pupil	loss per pupil totalling 3 or less school days	loss per pupil totalling 4-10 school days	loss per pupil totalling 11-20 school days	loss per pupil totalling 21 or over school days
Central	a		✓		✓	✓	✓
	b					✓	✓
Fife	c	✓	✓		✓	✓	✓
Grampian	d				✓		
Highland	e	✓					✓
Lothian	f	✓	✓	✓	✓	✓	
	g	✓			✓		
	h			✓			
Strathclyde	i	✓			✓	✓	✓
	j	✓		✓			
	k	✓	✓	✓			
	l	✓	✓	✓			
	m	✓	✓	✓	✓		✓
	n	✓	✓	✓		✓	
	o		✓		✓		✓
	p			✓			
	q			✓			
	r			✓			
	s				✓		
Strathclyde Primaries	t	✓	✓		✓	✓	
	u	✓	✓	✓			
	v		✓				

Eight schools fell into the highest 10 per cent of users of single *and* of repeat exclusions. The headteachers of these schools all described the majority of their pupils as coming from 'disadvantaged' backgrounds. This was the only clear characteristic in common. As far as the loss of schooling suffered by their excluded pupils went, the pattern varied. Six of these eight schools were in the top 10 per cent of users of exclusions totalling three or fewer days. Two were in the top 10 per cent of users of exclusions totalling 21 or more days but one of them did not exclude anyone for this long. In other words, these schools were 'high' excluders as far as number of exclusions went but this did not necessarily mean they were also 'high' excluders in terms of the amount of schooling lost by these pupils.

Another way of thinking about what a 'high' excluding school means is a school that uses exclusions repeatedly in response to difficulties evinced by the same pupil. Nine schools in our survey which completed the report form had excluded pupils repeatedly more often than they excluded pupils once. There was no single characteristic which all nine schools had in common; however, different combinations of the schools meant that seven of the nine schools were from Strathclyde Education Authority, were secondary schools, had above their regional average for authorised absence, and emphasised the importance of exclusion as minimising the disruption to the teaching and learning of the other pupils. The headteachers of five of the nine schools described the majority of the pupils as having 'disadvantaged' backgrounds. It is worth emphasising that although most excluded *pupils* were excluded only once, yet of the 120 *schools* in our sample which returned details of their excluded pupils, only 19 had not used repeated exclusion of at least one pupil. Further, all schools in the highest 10 per cent of users of *any* of these variables used repeat exclusion but 11 of the schools in the lowest 10 per cent of users did *not* use repeat exclusion. This suggests that while it is the experience of many schools across Scotland that the 'short, sharp shock' of a single exclusion is not effective in changing the behaviour of certain pupils, low excluding schools found single exclusions more effective than schools making frequent use of exclusion.

Looking at the number of exclusions (times excluded) is one way of defining high exclusion; another way is to look at the loss of school days per excluded pupil. Of the 120 sample schools, 63 had excluded at least one pupil for a total of 21 days or more during the eight months covered by the form. Interestingly, just two of these schools *only* excluded pupil for this long and these two schools were not what might be thought of as stereotypical high excluding schools; rather they were schools which found themselves unable to deal with one or two pupils displaying serious behavioural problems. On the other hand, the six schools falling into the top 10 per cent of users of this variable were, perhaps, more like stereotypical high excluding schools. They all had below average regional or divisional results for 3+ Highers at A–C grade in S5. (See Appendix 1 for an explanation of the terms used in the Scottish education system.) Other than that, in various combinations, five of the six schools described the socio-economic status of the majority of their pupils as 'disadvantaged', had above average rates of authorised and unauthorised absence, and had below average staying on rates into S5. Yet three of these six schools described the normal pattern of pupil behaviour as 'generally accept-able, a few minor incidents or problems'. This suggests, perhaps, that one reason for their appearance as a high long-term excluding school was that dealing with a small number of particular pupils presented problems for these schools, too.

Rather than defining high exclusion either in terms of times excluded or loss of school days, we decided also to look at schools which fell into the top 10 per cent of four or more of the six variables. There were seven of these 'multiple high' excluding schools. There was no factor which all seven schools shared but six of the seven described their majority pupil socio-economic status as 'disadvan-taged'. The seventh school described its pupil socio-economic status as 'neutral'.

Taking together all these different ways of defining a high exclud-ing school, the single factor which might be most commonly shared is the description of pupil socio-economic status as 'disadvantaged'. However, not all the high excluding schools described their pupil socio-economic status in this way. Therefore, before concluding that this was indeed a critical factor we decided to look closely at schools which could be described as 'low' excluders and at those reporting no official exclusions.

Low excluding schools

As with high exclusion, low exclusion can also be defined in differ-ent ways. For example, one way of defining low exclusion is not excluding any pupils more than once. Six schools fell into the lowest 10 per cent of users of single exclusions *and* did not use repeat ex-clusions. As far as loss of schooling went, four of these schools excluded pupils for totals of between four and 10 school days only, they did not exclude pupils for other lengths of time. The other two schools excluded pupils for three days or less. Thus these schools were low excluders in terms of times excluded but not necessarily the lowest in terms of schooling lost.

The brevity of exclusion is itself a way of defining low exclusion. There were ten schools altogether which could be thought of as low excluders because exclusions lasted for a total of three or fewer school days. Eight of these schools described their pupil socio-economic status as 'relatively prosperous' or as 'neutral'; only one described it as 'disadvantaged'. All these schools described the normal pattern of pupil behaviour as either 'generally acceptable, a few minor incidents or problems' or as 'mostly acceptable, but a few serious incidents'. The number of pupils excluded was also very small – between one and three pupils. Thus it could be argued that perhaps these schools were low excluders not because of anything proactive but simply because they were located in good catchment areas with few difficult pupils. However, it was noticeable that eight of the headteachers mentioned the importance of involving parents, of their role in preventing exclusion and in ensuring the effectiveness of exclusion.

Interestingly, these 10 schools were remarkably similar to the two schools characterised as 'high' excluders because their excluded pupils had all lost 21 or more school days. Of course, school practice may explain this but to us the difference in this case between a 'high' or 'low' exclusion rate seemed to relate more to the severity of the problems displayed by a few pupils than to characteristics associated with these particular schools.

We also looked at a group of schools which could be thought of as low excluding ones because none of their excluded pupils had lost more than 20 school days *and* they were in the lowest 10 per cent of at least two of the other variables relating to times excluded or schooling lost. This group of 12 schools had a number of characteristics in common. All described the normal pattern of pupil behaviour as 'generally acceptable' or as 'mostly acceptable', 11 described their pupil socio-economic status as 'prosperous' or as 'neutral', the twelfth as 'mixed'. In addition, all emphasised the early or additional involvement of parents as important in preventing exclusion.

Thus we can say that low excluding schools, defined in different ways, tended to have in common an acceptable pattern of pupil behaviour, a prosperous or neutral majority pupil socio-economic status and an emphasis on the importance of parental involvement both in preventing exclusions and in making exclusion an effective sanction.

Schools reporting no exclusions

In our sample, 25 schools reported no official exclusions, of which 21 were primary schools and four were secondary schools. We divided these schools into two groups: one group of nine schools which had given us more than three strategies which they used to maintain pupils on the verge of exclusion, and one group of 16 schools which had given us three or fewer strategies for maintaining such pupils.

All nine schools reporting no official exclusions and offering more than three strategies were primary schools and all nine emphasised the importance of keeping pupils in school and of not excluding. Perhaps as a reflection of this emphasis, seven of them kept no central school record of exclusions other than what was asked for by the education authority. They also all had low numbers of pupils unofficially 'sent home' or perceived as on the verge of exclusion – mainly three or fewer. Pupil behaviour was perceived as normally 'generally acceptable' or 'mostly acceptable' in eight of the schools; in the ninth it was described as 'low level disruption and serious behaviour problems'. In terms of majority pupil socio-economic status, however, the schools varied: four described their socio-economic status as 'neutral', three as 'disadvantaged', one as 'prosperous' and one as 'mixed'. The number of strategies they offered as helping to prevent exclusion suggested that they were schools which were proactively trying to minimise exclusion. Again, one common theme was the involvement of parents in preventing exclusion.

None of the group of 16 schools reporting three or fewer strategies to combat exclusion described their socio-economic status as 'disadvantaged'. However, in other respects, this group was very like the group of nine. Most said their socio-economic status was 'neutral', the others 'mixed' or 'prosperous'. All described their normal pattern of pupil behaviour as 'generally acceptable' or 'mostly acceptable'. This was borne out by the fact that only one school unofficially 'sent home' pupils (n=2) and none perceived themselves as having more than two pupils on the verge of exclusion. These schools may, then, have had no exclusions because they were lucky enough to be sited in areas which were not disadvantaged and to have generally well behaved pupils. Yet in the schools which had pupils on the verge of exclusion, again the interviewees emphasised the importance of parental involvement. Other things were mentioned also but this strategy was the one most commonly cited.

To sum up: the low excluding schools, however this was defined, and the schools reporting no official exclusions during the time covered by the report form tended to be fairly similar in a number of ways, perhaps most notably, the emphasis on the importance of parental involvement and the descriptions of pupil socio-economic status as not being disadvantaged. By contrast, the high excluding schools, defined in different ways, tended to appear less like each other save that most, though not all, described their pupil socio-economic status as 'disadvantaged'. The high excluding schools in terms of days lost were alike in having below average examination results and below average attendance rates.

Summary

This chapter has considered the extent of exclusion, drawing attention to the steady rise in the numbers of permanent exclusions in England since 1993/94 and the 45 per cent increase in permanent exclusion from primary school between 1993/94 and 1995/96. Information about pupils excluded from Scottish schools was presented and reasons for exclusion given. The high number of pupils excluded for fighting and for rule breaking draws attention to the potentially positive effects on the disciplinary climate of schools, of playground projects and attention being paid to the school's physical environment, as well as of the genuine involvement of pupils in decisions about rules, rewards and sanctions.

Finally, characteristics of high and low excluding schools were described from our research. High excluding schools tended to be characterised as having a majority of pupils from areas of social and economic deprivation. Those which excluded pupils for 21 days or longer also tended to have lower than average examination results and attendance rates. Low excluding schools were similar in stressing the importance of parental involvement and in characterising their pupils as coming from 'neutral' or advantaged areas. It has long been recognised that the social and economic status of pupils, the composition of a school's population, has a profound effect on many aspects of school life, including attainment, truancy, discipline and staying on rates. Powerful though this influence is, it is not sufficient as an explanation for different practices among schools. Research has shown that schools with very similar pupil populations (advantaged, mixed, disadvantaged) vary in the use they make of exclusion. A key factor is that nebulous concept of school ethos, and as part of that, the beliefs of senior school staff about the purpose of schooling. This finding emerged strongly too from our case studies of matched pairs of schools with different exclusion rates. The importance of a positive ethos as a way of avoiding the need for exclusion is discussed in Chapter 4. First, however, we consider why schools exclude pupils and whether the current policy context promotes or constrains exclusion.

As a coda to the topic of measuring exclusion, it is worth adding that about 75 per cent of secondary schools in our survey collated school-level data on exclusions. Most used the data to establish trends over time, to evaluate and review policy or procedures and to monitor or support the school discipline system. The remainder largely used the data as information to be passed on in the school handbook, or to members of staff or to parents. There was, however, wide variation in the kind of data collected. Some schools, for example, did not record ethnicity or Record of needs (statement in England) information. The increasing emphasis on school self-evaluation in Scotland, together with a national form on which to record exclusion as part of the annual school census, should help provide a better basis for schools to reflect on the effectiveness of their policy and practice. It should also encourage education authorities to review exclusion rates across schools, to investigate both high and low excluding schools and to identify good practice which can be shared.

3

Policy Matters

We should be extremely careful about offering easy solutions or
suggesting that education can solve the problems of poverty.

(Glennerster, 1998)

A key feature of the Labour government's social policy is that of tackling social exclusion. In essence this is a multi-dimensional approach
to tackling poverty, disadvantage and disaffection. It is summed up
in the following way by Leney (1999:36):

It concerns institutional processes, a range of factors and the individual's own experience at different moments in the life cycle. And
policies to address social exclusion involve, at least, access to
employment that can be sustained, access to education, training
and skills, changes in the housing sector, improved standards of
living . . .

For the purposes of this chapter the focus is on policy affecting access
to education or, more properly, access to schooling – although we
recognise that schooling is part of a larger social and economic context and we return to a consideration of the role of the school in combating social exclusion in the final chapter.

In particular the chapter describes the main features of current legislation on exclusion from school, highlighting the distinctive differences between Scotland and England. It then considers the policy and
practice dilemmas faced by schools as they seek both to raise pupils'
standards of attainment and to promote access to schooling. Firstly,
however, it briefly reviews the main themes from research that indicate the different views that people might hold about disaffected
behaviour in school.

31

Explanations of disaffected behaviour

Underpinning policy and practice on exclusion from school are explanations of the causes of disaffected behaviour and hence of the appropriate response to it. Broadly speaking explanations fall into two categories, those which locate 'causes' within the individual child and family and those which locate 'causes' in society in general and in schools as organisations. In the past most explanations were rooted in the individual child who was seen as either 'mad' or 'bad' and so requiring either sustained medical or psychiatrically based intervention or punishment (Bridgeland, 1971). Often the best that could be done was to provide some form of containment. As Sandow (1994:2) makes clear, 'The implication of such a view is that education for the affected child is impossible and may be almost sacrilegious: "flying in the face of nature." ' Contemporary explanations include the neo biological, used for example to explain the behaviour of children who show an apparently abnormal incapacity for sustained attention. Labels like attention deficit and hyperactivity disorder are increasingly used by teachers and psychologists to explain problem behaviour (Armstrong and Galloway, 1994; Ferguson *et al.*, 1997). Thus one strand of response to disaffected behaviour is to 'do something' about the individual young person. Interventions range from drug therapy for Attention Deficit Hyperactivity Disorder to psychological and psychiatric treatments. Therapeutic approaches in school are described in Chapter 6.

A wide range of research studies has pointed to the influence of school effects on behaviour. Such studies include the large-scale and statistically robust research on school effectiveness (e.g. Rutter *et al.*, 1979; Reynolds, 1997; Sammons *et al.*, 1997) as well as in-depth qualitative studies of small numbers of schools and pupils (e.g. Hargreaves *et al.*, 1975; Munn *et al.*, 1992a, 1992b; Jones and Jones, 1992; Ruddock *et al.*, 1996). These studies show that schools (and departments and teachers) make a difference. Schools with pupils from similar backgrounds can vary in their effectiveness in terms of pupils' behaviour, achievement and attendance, and much else besides. These studies attempt to identify the various aspects of schools which, taken together, make a difference. They include:

• the physical environment being made welcoming and comfortable;
• pupils' work valued through regular displays which are updated regularly;
• positive teacher–pupil relationships incorporating high teacher expectations of pupils' academic and other achievements;

- personal and social development given a high priority;
- homework set and marked regularly;
- active leadership and a shared vision of what the school is aiming to do;
- pupil participation in decision-making about school and classroom life.

Taken together, these elements are generally regarded as a school's *ethos* or culture. These studies, therefore, suggest that there are things schools can do to influence the behaviour of pupils. Interventions on school ethos are described in more detail in Chapter 4.

Cooper and Upton (1990; Upton and Cooper, 1990; Cooper, 1996) highlight the usefulness of the 'ecosystemic approach' with young people exhibiting emotional and behavioural difficulties. As the label suggests, the approach focuses on systems at school and in the environment of the young person in ways which 'are compatible with the humanistic aims of education, which are to facilitate the development of autonomy and self direction in students, and in ways that do not appear to shift the blame for emotional and behavioural difficulties from pupils to their teachers and parents' (Cooper and Upton, 1991:22).

Policy and guidance on school exclusion reveal the tensions in the explanations for disaffection. These include the individualisation of reasons for challenging behaviour and the consequent need for interventions or treatment targeted at the individual young people. Within this research literature there have also been attempts to categorise more precisely than hitherto the diverse nature of social, emotional and behavioural difficulties exhibited by pupils. These challenge the usefulness of social, emotional and behavioural difficulties as a category. This has resulted in some authors suggesting that some categories of pupils with social, emotional and behavioural difficulties are authors of their own misfortune and therefore deserve punishment, while others have intrinsic social, emotional and behavioural difficulties which deserves therapy or other forms of treatment (see Munn and Lloyd forthcoming for a review). The tension between punishment and treatment is evident in exclusions legislation as we shall see below. Policy and guidance also include the encouragement to schools to work with other agencies to support young people in trouble and for schools to develop a more positive and caring ethos.

Avoiding inappropriate blame

It is all too easy to blame schools, social work services or psychological services for failing young people. It is equally easy for schools and the like to blame the individual young person for anti-social behaviour. This individualisation process, whether to institutions or people, diverts attention from structural inequalities in terms of wealth, and so of housing, health and educational opportunity. When Halsey was writing in 1972 about the introduction of Educational Priority Areas he argued that we should avoid treating education as a waste paper basket of social policy, as a way of dealing with social problems where there seem to be no solutions. Similarly Hopmann and Konzuli (1997), reflecting on schooling in Sweden but conscious of its similarities to many other Western countries, claim that common social problems which are difficult to resolve have come to be blamed on schools with little thought about what is appropriate or realistic to expect of schools, or the purposes for which schools are actually resourced.

Current policies to tackle social exclusion seem to recognise that schools are only part of the jigsaw, albeit an important one in developing a more inclusive society. As subsequent chapters reveal, there is a great deal that schools are already doing to provide good quality alternatives to exclusion. The broader approach under the banner of tackling social exclusion is untested but it is an overdue and welcome recognition of the need for school policy to be integrated into broader social policy development.

English legislation on exclusion

Exclusions were first regulated in England by the 1986 Education (No. 2) Act and subsequent Acts have amended or added to its provisions (Parsons, 1999). There are broadly three categories of exclusion: permanent exclusion where a pupil is removed from the register of the school; temporary or fixed term exclusion where a pupil is not permitted to attend school for a specified length of time and then re-admitted; and informal exclusion where pupils are sent home for a few days to 'cool off' but this is not officially recorded on the pupil's file.

Concerns about the rising levels of permanent and fixed term exclusions in England together with the Labour government's commitment to tackle social exclusion in general have resulted in a new series of measures designed to tackle exclusion from school. These are seen as one aspect of policy to promote social inclusion.

The main measures to tackle permanent and fixed term exclusion from school are (Social Exclusion Unit, 1998):

- The setting up of national targets to reduce by one-third numbers of both fixed term and permanent exclusions from school by 2002.
- All pupils excluded from school for more than three weeks will

receive alternative full-time and appropriate education, supported by an individual learning plan which includes a target date for reintegration into mainstream schooling.

- LEAs are required to set targets for the reduction of permanent exclusion from September 1999 and of fixed term exclusions from September 2000. These should be set out in LEAs' Education Development Plans.
- The government will publish data on performance on exclusion down to school level for secondary schools and LEA level for primary schools. Performance data sheets should be broken down by ethnic group since the problem of exclusions of ethnic minorities is so serious.
- Exclusion for minor offences/incidents is illegal.
- There are plans to change the procedures for calculating the performance tables (of pupils' attainments) to ensure that exclusion cannot be used as a device for manipulating the reported figures.
- Ofsted will conduct special inspections of ten schools each year which have disproportionately high levels of exclusion (and truancy). (Local authorities can also ask Ofsted to investigate if they have similar concerns and independent appeal panels can draw to the attention of the LEA concerns they have about high excluding schools.)
- LEAs will be encouraged to give schools 'dowries' as a support package to receive a pupil who has been excluded from another school and to support children at risk of exclusion.

These features are markedly different in tone and intent from earlier legislation which highlighted the importance of exclusion as a sanction to promote good order and discipline.

In addition, and in keeping with the current emphasis on work to minimise the risk of exclusion, LEAs must publish behaviour support plans, setting out arrangements for tackling pupils' behaviour and discipline problems. New money has been made available from the Excellence Fund for authorities to develop innovative and imaginative alternatives to exclusion. This drive to reduce exclusion exists in a legislative context in which:

- the headteacher of a maintained school may exclude a pupil from the school for a fixed period or permanently;
- the maximum permissible period of fixed term exclusion is 45 days and this maximum may be used in one term;
- the headteacher must inform the LEA and the governing body where the pupil would, as a result of any exclusion, be excluded

from school for a total of more than five school days in any one term, or lose an opportunity to take any public examination; or when the school excludes a pupil permanently;

- the school's governing body shall i) consider the circumstances in which a pupil was excluded and ii) consider any representation made to it by the excluded pupil or the parent/carer and by the LEA;
- where practical the governing body is to give a direction to the headteacher requiring the reinstatement of a pupil (this includes dates for reinstatement or permanent exclusion);
- the parent of a pupil who has been permanently excluded twice is an 'unfit person' and loses the right to choose the school his/her child will attend.

Decisions to exclude a pupil are typically taken in the first instance by the headteacher or a senior colleague and ratified by the school's governing body, which is also empowered to hear representations against exclusion and to give direction to the headteacher regarding the reinstatement of the excluded pupil. Parents/carers and young people over 18 years of age have the right to appeal to a local education authority panel against a decision to exclude. Parents can further appeal for a judicial review on one or more of the following grounds: a failure to follow the correct procedures, an error of law or breach of an implied limitation, typically a lack of fairness or fair-mindedness in the school which excluded the complainant. Parsons (1999:121) gives examples of these kinds of appeals but cautions that 'the best that an excluded child can obtain from the court is a quashing of the head's/governors' decision and an opportunity for the decision taker to decide again in a more fair-minded or procedurally correct way. Whether this will give the applicant what he or she really wants is another matter.'

Scottish legislation on exclusion

In contrast, in Scotland there has been no legislation on exclusion since 1982 when the 1975 Schools General (Scotland) Regulations were amended. The Scottish Office issued *Guidance on Issues Concerning Exclusion from School* in 1998 (2/98) which emphasises the use of exclusion as a last resort, points out the illegality of informal exclusion and requires local councils to collect statistics on exclusion. In brief, the power to exclude – and so legal responsibility for exclusion – rests with the education authority. It is, however, open to an authority to devolve the ability to exclude to school level. Key features are:

- Grounds of exclusion are i) that the pupil's continued attendance at school is seriously detrimental to order and discipline or the educational well-being of pupils there; ii) the parent of the pupil refuses or fails to comply, or to allow the pupil to comply, with the rules, regulations or disciplinary requirements of the school.
- The length of the exclusion is not defined and accordingly is at the discretion of the education authority.
- The legislation does not make a distinction between temporary and permanent exclusion, although the terms are used by some authorities and schools. Some authorities, however, do not use the term permanent exclusion. They see it as inappropriate when the underlying approach is one of inclusion and because the education authority retains duties in relation to a child removed from the register of a particular school.
- For monitoring purposes, two terms, 'temporary exclusion' and 'exclusion/removal from the register', should be used.
- Parents/carers may appeal against an exclusion to an appeal committee set up by the education authority and subsequently to the sheriff.
- Citing the United Nations Convention on the Rights of the Child, to which the UK is a signatory, the Guidance (2/98 para 7) stipulates that 'a pupil facing exclusion should always be given the opportunity to express a view and should have that view taken into account'.
- Exclusion is a last resort and the Guidance (2/98 para 53) states that 'it is only in very exceptional circumstances that a pupil is excluded from a school and removed from the register without a clear plan for appropriate alternative provision being established beforehand and without supportive intervention having already been undertaken, frequently involving collaboration with other agencies'.
- Permission to depart from national curriculum guidelines in planned ways to address the specific needs of an individual pupil.

Scottish/English differences

Thus there are important differences in the Scottish and English legislative frameworks surrounding exclusion from school, although each may be seen as attempting to reduce exclusions by setting a tone in which exclusion is seen as a last resort and the duty of the (L)EA to make full time educational provision for young people who have been excluded is stressed. These differences are summarised in Table 3.1.

While direct statistical comparisons on permanent exclusions between the two countries are misleading, since some Scottish local authorities do not recognise permanent exclusions, the figures quoted by Parsons (1999) are striking. Some 343 pupils, 0.042 per cent of the total Scottish school population, were permanently excluded in 1994/95 compared with 12,458, 0.159 per cent of the English school population (Parsons, 1999: 33). Parsons contends that exclusions were largely created as a consequence of the introduction of quasi-market approaches to school provision and hence to increasing competition among schools to attract and retain high achieving pupils. If this is so then the lower exclusion rates in Scotland may partly be explained by the less vigorous application of quasi-market principles to schools and the resistance of the Scottish education policy community to those that were invoked, which in turn may explain the lack of legislation

Table 3.1.   English–Scottish legislative differences on exclusion

	England	*Scotland*
Length of fixed term exclusion stipulated?	Yes – 45 days in one term.	No – at education authorities' discretion. Local policy varies but no national maximum specified.
Governors/school board members involved?	Yes – must approve permanent exclusions, receive representations and instruct on terms for excluded pupil's reinstatement.	No – headteacher or other senior member of staff. Education authority notified but policy varies on when to do so.
Permanent exclusion accepted?	Yes	Not by all education authorities.
Parents'/carers' right of appeal?	Yes – to local authority, and to judicial review.	Yes – to local authority and to sheriff.
Local authority behaviour support plans mandatory?	Can make representation to governing body.	No – guidance on key features of policy and practice.
Parental rights of choice of school affected?	Yes – after pupil has been permanently excluded from two schools.	No.

on exclusion (McPherson and Raab, 1988; Munn, 1997; Paterson, 1997).

While national legislative frameworks provide the backdrop against which exclusion takes place, there is clearly a major role for local education authorities in supporting and enabling schools to maintain pupils in mainstream schools. The publication of behaviour support plans 'to ensure that LEAs have coherent, comprehensive and well-understood local arrangements for tackling pupils' behaviour and discipline problems that cover the full range of needs' (DfEE, 1/98) is designed to encourage strategic thinking at local level and to model good practice in the development of plans. Research reviewing 61 Behaviour Support Plans (BSPs) in England revealed huge differences in the policy and practices of local education authorities towards children who are excluded from school. 'Some plans are excellent and should be commended for their readability, description of the issues, presentations of statistics and comprehensiveness. Other plans lack coherence, do not give any or enough data on the scale of the problem, are not based on consultation, fail to identify issues for improvement and have equal opportunities implications' (Rathbone, 1999). The research pointed out that some plans were not written in user friendly language and would be difficult for parents to read and understand.

Our Scottish research, undertaken before the establishment of 32 unitary authorities in 1996, revealed wide variation among the 12 Regional Authorities in terms of the comprehensiveness of policies on exclusion, collection of statistics and routine monitoring of out-of-school provision (Munn *et al.*, 1997). The main areas of diversity were:

- informal exclusion, where pupils were sent home for a 'cooling off' period without any record of such an event being kept. Four authorities permitted this at the time of the research either explicitly or implicitly; three expressly forbade it and five made no mention of it in policy documents.
- permanent exclusion, where the pupil could not be readmitted to the original school. This was a feature of policy in only three authorities, although other authorities accepted exclusion plus transfer to another school – in effect a permanent exclusion from the original school.
- notification of exclusion to the authority. Five authorities wanted notification of all exclusions while seven required notification only of exclusions of a certain number of days or beyond.
- stages of exclusion. These included 'at the headteacher's

discretion'; two types such as 'under 14 days' and '14 days and over'; three stages of varying lengths, e.g. 5/10/15 days, 5/15/30 days.

- volume and, by implication, status of policy. Some authorities had fairly voluminous documentation and referred to other policies such as those for special educational needs. Others deliberately eschewed a formal policy statement, relying instead on a standard letter to headteachers.
- policy aims – all authorities stressed that exclusion was a serious step and should be used as a last resort. However, ten authorities emphasised the overall aim of inclusion, sustaining pupils in mainstream schools; two emphasised the need for accurate record keeping and adherence to the authority's procedures with an eye on legal process.
- status of an excluded child pending an appeal. In some authorities the pupil remained excluded when an appeal was lodged even if the appeal took place at a time after the pupil could have been readmitted.

The main areas of similarity among most, but not all, authorities were:

- the lack of a systematic collation and analysis of exclusion statistics and hence of a strategic overview in terms of schools, or of pupil characteristics such as age, gender, ethnic origin, special needs or whether the case was referable to the Children's Panel (see Appendix 2 for an explanation of the Children's Hearing System in Scotland).
- the lack of a strategic overview of the range, quality and cost of alternative, off-site provision, regularly monitored, up-dated and debated.
- the ad hoc provision of staff development in the area of pupils with social, emotional and behavioural difficulties.

The Alternatives to Exclusion Grant scheme and money made available under the Excellence Fund to ensure that appropriate provision can be made for pupils who have been excluded or are at risk of exclusion emphasises the role of local authorities in supporting and working with schools. Many innovative and imaginative schemes are under way, ranging from the Building Bridges project run by Perth and Kinross Council in the north, focusing on supporting pupils through the transition from primary to secondary schools using peer support, individual education plans and parent support groups, to the KWESI project in Birmingham run by black men supporting those judged to be vulnerable to exclusion which provides mentoring support for African-Caribbean boys. The KWESI project has seen exclusion rates falling by 23 per cent with two-thirds of the reduction comprising ethnic minority pupils (Social Exclusion Unit, 1998; Osler and Hill, 1999).

A good deal of dedicated and imaginative work to tackle exclusion is taking place. Government recognition of exclusion from school as a serious issue is welcome; so too is the commitment to tackle it by setting a tone through legislation and guidance which discourages the too ready use of exclusion as a sanction and embeds this in a broader social policy context of reducing child poverty and social exclusion. Many local authorities are engaged in schemes to reduce exclusion from school and, as will be seen in successive chapters, many schools make unstinting efforts to sustain young people in mainstream education. Yet there are many dilemmas of policy and practice confronting those who wish to reduce or eliminate exclusion. Dilemmas by their nature have no easy resolution. Articulating them here is one way of encouraging teachers, local and national policy makers and parent and other community organisations to reflect on them and to consider their best way of resolving them.

Dilemmas of policy and practice

This section begins by focusing on some policy and practice dilemmas faced by the school in terms of exclusion. School is the place where decisions are taken to exclude a young person and so an exploration of some of the dilemmas facing schools is an important starting point in considering the extent to which local and national policies to reduce exclusion will take root.

Schools may be understood as institutions driven by diverse and contested purposes, by the values of those who go there and by the practices which may or may not reflect purposes and values. Thus when it comes to decisions on exclusion, competing claims have to be weighed and compromises reached. Few people involved in exclusion from school, at whatever level, see it as straightforward and unproblematic. Four main dilemmas are highlighted by way of illustrating one part of the terrain in which a policy to tackle exclusion will operate.

Conflicting goals

School discipline has always served two purposes. Good discipline is a *means to an end*, the end being to create the conditions for pupils to learn. It is fairly self evident that pupils cannot learn in a disorderly and unsafe classroom or school. Of course we are not suggesting here that good discipline guarantees effective learning, many factors contribute to this including pupils' motivation, their previous learning, the resources available and so on. Nevertheless good classroom and school discipline is an important ingredient in the factors affecting learning. Good discipline, however, is also *an end in itself*. Schools play an inescapable role in the socialisation of pupils. This has been so for as long as schools have been in existence. Thus in the early seventeenth century for example:

> The 1675 Synod of Aberdeen asked its presbyteries only to demand three questions of the school master: whether he makes the bairns learn the catechism, whether he teaches them prayers for morning and evening and grace for meals and whether 'he chastise them for cursing, swearing, lying, speaking profanietie for disobedience to parents and what vices that appears in them'.
>
> (Simpson quoted in Smout, 1969:84)

More recently Barber (1996:187–188) comments:

> If we want young people to learn the rules of living and working in communities – how to solve differences of opinion, how to respect a variety of beliefs . . . then these must feature in the curriculum of schools.

The inherent dilemmas for schools of pursuing these twin purposes are evident in the current policy context. On the one hand the importance of discipline as a means to an end can be seen in the drive to raise standards of pupils' attainment as measured in national tests, public examination results and international comparisons. Furthermore the publication of school performance tables, giving details of the relative attainments of pupils in schools across the UK, provide a very clear mechanism of public accountability for schools. It therefore, seems entirely logical for schools to seek to maximise their position on such tables, especially when a further mechanism of public accountability is the right for parents to choose the schools their children will attend. On the other hand, schools are being discouraged from excluding pupils, pupils who might well be seen as threatening attainment targets because of disruptive behaviour in classrooms. The resolution of this dilemma might be the greater use of internal exclusion which camouflages the extent of disaffection and also raises questions about the quality of schooling on offer (see Chapter 4).

Similarly schools are being given mixed messages about how they should view pupils. The Children's Act (1989) and the Children (Scotland) Act (1995) stress a welfare principle, the best interests of the child, and delineate children's rights to be consulted about and participate in decisions which directly affect them. Education legislation carries no such imperatives (Parsons, 1999). As Parsons further points out (1999:7).

> Childhood activity, and roles proper for it, are social constructions, varying across national cultures and history. We see child workers in the Indian subcontinent and gun-toting 12-year-olds in Africa. In the UK, probably more than other countries in the 'developed' west, children have no legitimate voice.

It is noteworthy for instance that in recent legislation such as the 1997 Education Act and the 1998 School Standards and Framework Act 'the quantity of text . . . devoted to regulating the process of exclusion and establishing judicial and ever more complex procedures for appeal, overshadowed any text relating to the needs of the child or the child's access to full-time education' (Parsons, 1999:108). We contend that this approach differs from that adopted in Scotland where there has been no flurry of legislation relating to exclusion and national guidance on exclusion (Scottish Office, 1998) is congruent with the child welfare emphasis underpinning the Scottish approach to youth offending.

Collective and individual welfare

There are, furthermore, the competing claims of the rights of the individual disruptive child or young person to schooling weighed against the claims of the majority of pupils to enjoy a safe and secure educational environment and not to be distracted from work by disruptive behaviour. Teachers and others are aware of the time and effort which can be devoted to a small number of disaffected pupils, time which is, therefore, being denied the majority. The competing claims of individual and collective welfare rights are beginning to be tackled in cases of young people with special educational needs. In the past it was rare for these young people to be educated in mainstream schools; they were typically educated in specialist day or residential provision or in special units attached to mainstream schools. That situation is gradually changing and there is now a more varied population of children with special needs in both mainstream and special schools (Allan *et al.*, 1995) although the figure of 1.2 per cent of all school pupils educated in special schools has changed little over the years (Closs, 1997). In contrast, the special school population declined in England in 1996 to 1.4 per cent of all 5–15-year-olds, the lowest ever percentage for England (Norwich, 1997), although there are wide variations across local education authorities in the percentages of pupils they place in special schools. Norwich (1997) identifies a range from 0.32 per cent in Newham to 2.31 per cent in Hackney. The practice of assessing and recording or statementing children with special educational needs is now well established although problematic in practice (Thomson *et al.*, 1996). Yet recording/statementing remains an important vehicle promoting entitlement to specialist provision for young people in need. The more recent adoption of Individual Education Plans (IEPs) and the current advocacy of Personal Learning Plans (PLPs) for all children (Scottish Office, 1999) may be a useful way of a) encouraging teachers to see children with behavioural difficulties as having special needs and worthy of support in much the same way as other children with special needs and b) identifying the specialist help and other resources needed to meet their needs. This approach, however, is not without its problems. Petrie and Shaw (1998:123) confirm that the needs based approach reduces whole groups of people:

> to bundles of need – deficit individuals requiring help without anything to offer – objects rather than active subjects.

Writing about the struggle for inclusion they contend that professionals can conceptualise their role as a series of technical challenges to overcome barriers to the inclusion of those with special needs. Rather, the concern should be 'to shift the discourse of disability from one of "in-person" deficiency to one of discrimination and rights' (Petrie and Shaw, 1998:124). As we shall see in successive chapters many schools have begun to shift from individual deficit explanations as the only way of understanding challenging behaviour. We are, however, still far away from establishing a rights agenda for pupils who are excluded from school, although recent Scottish guidance on exclusion mentioned above (Scottish Office, 1998) signals such a move. Even if teachers can be encouraged to see troubled and troublesome youngsters as having special needs, however, there remains the question of where these needs might be met and also who should do so.

Even if headteachers do not massage the figures a low exclusion rate may conceal poor quality provision for pupils in trouble, such as sitting in corridors or other forms of 'internal exclusion' (see Chapter 5). Thus ways of affirming the broad range of the purposes of schooling need to be found in addition to performance management systems. More fundamentally, however, the aspects of schooling concerned with pupils' cognitive attainments, as certificated by public examinations, confer distinct advantages to those possessing such certificates over those who do not possess them. Public examination certificates are the gateway to further and higher education and to the labour market. Access to these opportunities is competitive. Thus things which stand in the way of pupils maximising their chances of securing good examination results are bound to be resisted by pupils themselves and especially parents, who are aware of the advantages good results can bring. Schools can be under significant pressure from parents to exclude children who are perceived as threatening the opportunity of other children to succeed as well as their safety and general welfare. Thus schools wanting to reduce or eliminate exclusions face very real dilemmas about the balance of effort devoted to individual as opposed to collective welfare. In matters of safety and well being collective welfare will always take precedence over individual welfare.

Professional autonomy

A third dilemma concerns the professional autonomy of teachers and headteachers. A consistent approach to classroom discipline across a range of subjects and staff in a large secondary school is no easy matter even where staff are inclined to adopt such an approach. The private nature of teaching, the professional autonomy of the individual teacher in the day-to-day management of the classroom and the context specific nature of discipline, all make consistency a goal which has to be continually reaffirmed. Many schools are adopting policies highlighting praise and reward for good behaviour which can open up discussion among staff and pupils about what counts as good behaviour and about how to promote positive relationships between staff and pupils. This kind of approach, as well as staff analysing patterns of 'referral' and exclusion of pupils, is beginning to show some positive results (Munn, 1999b). Yet the private nature of much teaching can make it difficult for headteachers to be seen to be fair to both staff and pupils in using exclusion as a sanction. It is noteworthy that almost all excluded pupils interviewed in research studies say that they have been treated unfairly. 'They would say that, wouldn't they' is an easy reaction from stressed or cynical staff. Yet sufficient is known about the negative effects of labelling pupils as disruptive to raise questions about consistency and justice in the use of exclusions (see Chapter 1).

National and local policy can help put structures in place to promote justice. Local authorities, for instance, can require a series of steps to be taken before exclusion, such as consultation with and the provision of reports from educational psychologists, which constrain the power of a headteacher to exclude a child for more than three days. Headteachers themselves may draw up procedures to discourage staff from using exclusion, such as meetings with guidance staff, social workers and others to assess the needs of the child and determine ways of meeting these. Structures and procedures alone, however, are insufficient. The nature of teacher and of headteacher autonomy means that procedures and structures can be subverted, sometimes in a bid to access scarce resources, sometimes as a way of obtaining respite from a difficult pupil. Policies, structures and procedures need to be underpinned by a sense of belief and support for their aims. Caught up as they are with the day-to-day realities of teaching and managing schools, it can be difficult for teachers and headteachers to remind themselves of the broader social functions of schooling, the successes which the school system has delivered in terms of rising numbers of pupils achieving passes in public examinations. It is this kind of awareness that needs to be encouraged in initial teacher education and continued professional development programmes if the spirit as well as the letter of exclusion policy and guidelines is to be followed.

Curriculum Entitlement

Lastly, there is a dilemma about curriculum entitlement. In Scotland the 5–14 curriculum guidelines specify broad areas of knowledge to which all children should be exposed and suggest the proportions of time to be spent on these. Some flexibility in provision is permitted but this is usually seen as enhancing or reinforcing particular areas such as language or expressive arts, rather than reducing provision. Similarly the 14–16 curriculum sets out 'modes' which every pupil must study while permitting choice of particular subjects seen as fulfilling each mode. Where troubled behaviour has its roots in learning difficulties, questions immediately arise as to the appropriateness of the curriculum for pupils. Yet to restrict access can be seen as unduly disadvantaging pupils and even if a decision is taken to do so, questions remain about how to restrict access. Clear guidance from local and national government on this issue would help. Some teachers are afraid that they will be criticised by local authority evaluation and review teams and/or by the HMI if curriculum entitlement is restricted.

A related aspect concerns the prominence given by schools to traditional academic qualifications as compared with those which are more vocationally orientated and skills based. There is increasing recognition that traditional classroom-based teaching is not attractive to some young people and the Scottish Office is currently commissioning research on the effectiveness of extended work experience, enterprise education and other learning approaches in motivating disaffected young people and thereby helping tackle behaviour which leads to exclusion (SEED, 1999). The reform of upper secondary education in Scotland for 16–18-year-olds, Higher Still, with its emphasis on a unified system of academic and vocational provision through a single ladder of progression and attainment, and the more rapid accreditation of learning through units (Raffe, 1997) may help, particularly if it begins to replace the two year Standard Grade courses for 14–16-year-olds. The provision of courses below Higher level at Intermediate 1 and 2 makes this a distinct possibility.

In England and Wales, too, there has been a growing awareness of the links between disaffection and an overly prescriptive and academic curriculum (Kinder *et al.*, 1995; Dearing, 1996). As a result, schools have been enabled and encouraged to offer more choices at Key Stage 4 (i.e. for 14–16-year-old pupils) (G.B. DfEE, 1998; QCA, 1998; G.B. DfEE, 1999). Possibilities include, for example, spending more time on developing key skills, spending part of the week at college, in training or with an employer learning vocational or pre-vocational skills, or attending youth and/or community activities designed to promote personal and pro-social skills. Such alternative curriculum programmes, involving adapting the learning context and/or content for 14–16-year-olds in schools, when carefully set up, well run, monitored and evaluated, have been shown to be successful in preventing exclusions and in enabling young people to find suitable positive progression routes post-16 (Cullen *et al.*, forthcoming).

Conclusion

Schooling is an important component in tackling social exclusion both in terms of *prevention* – hence the government's emphasis on pre-school provision and on early intervention to combat children's difficulties in reading and number work, and in terms of *sustaining* young people in mainstream school through a raft of measures such as study support, adapted curricula and education action zones to 'turn around' schools with poor standards of performance. Within this range of policy initiatives there are specific measures regarding exclusion from school. These include Alternatives to Exclusion schemes through which schools and local education authorities are encouraged to develop innovative and interesting ways of maintaining in school young people displaying troubled or troublesome behaviour.

Policies promoting access to school and discouraging exclusion are part of a broader drive to improve pupils' standards of attainment as measured by national tests and public examination results. A key feature of the standards agenda under both the current Labour and previous Conservative administrations is a belief in the efficacy of a quasi-market approach in raising standards.

The combination of a quasi-market approach to school improvement together with legislation and guidance to reduce exclusion from school had inevitably resulted in a number of dilemmas for schools. The chapters which follow show how schools involved in our research resolved these to provide positive alternatives to exclusion from school.

4

Ethos and Exclusions

We are now a school which is 'Promoting Positive Behaviour' . . .
the focus of the staff is now on the positive ethos in the classroom.
(Secondary school teacher)

What is ethos?

The dictionary defines ethos as 'the guiding beliefs, standards
or ideals that characterise or pervade a group, a community, a
people . . . the spirit that motivates the ideas, customs or practices of
a people (Websters, 1986). This definition is helpful because it highlights first of all the *pervasive* nature of ethos. In a school, ethos
touches all aspects of its operation but its very pervasiveness means
that it is hard to pin down. Ethos is so much part and parcel of the
taken-for-granted about the way any school goes about its business
that it can be hard to describe. Secondly, the definition illuminates the
fact that ethos underpins our *practice*, what we do in schools and how
we do it. Thus ethos is not an abstract idea. It helps to explain why
we act in particular ways and so why our actions can be different
according to the particular school in which we work. Thirdly, the definition focuses on the idea of a group, a *collective understanding* of how
things are done. Ethos can refer to an individual's character, of course,
but for the purposes of this chapter the focus is upon the ethos of the
school as an entity.

School ethos, then, can help us understand why schools vary in
their approach to exclusion and indeed in other things too. It is now
generally recognised that schools make a difference. Schools with
similar kinds of pupils vary in their effectiveness as measured by
public examination results and in terms of other outcomes such as

49

attendance and behaviour. (See, for example, White and Barber, 1997; Sammons *et al.*, 1997; Gray *et al.*, 1996; Mortimore *et al.* 1988.) One of the earliest studies of school effectiveness, *Fifteen Thousand Hours* (Rutter *et al.*, 1979), highlighted the concept of school climate as helping to explain variation among schools in their effectiveness. More recent studies sustain this view (Bosker and Sheerens, 1994; Sammons *et al.*, 1997) although the particular elements which make up school climate are contested and little is known about how they interact. Likewise studies of school discipline stress the importance of the culture of the school in understanding why schools in similar neighbourhoods and with similar kinds of pupils vary in the way they tackle behaviour issues (Munn *et al.*, 1992a, 1992b; Slee, 1995; Charlton and David, 1993). If school ethos is a key to understanding differences among schools in their use of exclusion, then changing the ethos is a fundamental strategy to tackle exclusion. This is easier said than done, of course. We contend, however, that unless schools are willing to examine their ethos, exploring the values and beliefs which underpin their practices, they will not develop genuine alternatives to exclusion. They will be deploying short-term and relatively ineffective 'cures' to behaviour problems rather than tackling some root causes.

This chapter is in three parts. First, it uses examples from the case study schools involved in our research to illustrate ways in which a school's ethos influences its use of exclusion. Secondly, it describes some practical strategies which schools report as improving their general disciplinary climate, thereby helping to reduce the level of short-term exclusion. Such strategies can be a way into schools exploring their ethos. Thirdly, it reports a Scottish approach to sustaining schools' self examination of their ethos through an ethos network, involving teachers, parents, pupils, support staff and others sharing their experience and ideas. The network encourages schools to learn from each other about ways of researching their ethos and about how to take action to develop a more positive school climate. The chapter ends by suggesting that local authorities and/or groups of schools could develop their own ethos networks as a way of learning about each other's approaches to promoting a positive ethos and so help to tackle exclusion.

How does ethos affect exclusion?

In this section we take four key aspects of school ethos and describe how they influence exclusion. At the end of the section we summarise these aspects in terms of characteristics of schools which tend towards inclusion or exclusion of troubled and troublesome pupils. The examples are taken from the eight secondary schools and four primary schools involved in the case study phase of our research. The schools were roughly matched in pairs in terms of pupil characteristics (poor, prosperous etc); geographic location (city, suburban, rural); headteacher's views of normal patterns of pupil behaviour; numbers of pupils with Records of Need and numbers of pupils with significant but unrecorded learning difficulties. The schools differed, however, in the use they made of exclusion. Each pair consisted of a high excluding and a low excluding school. Our choice of low excluding schools was influenced by headteachers' reports from a larger survey on in-school strategies to prevent exclusion. We studied schools with lower exclusion which claimed to be making an effort to achieve this, rather than schools with no exclusions because they had a history of very few behaviour problems. We interviewed a small sample of staff, parents, pupils and educational psychologists and other education professionals in each school. We set out to explore the perceptions of the use of exclusion by asking respondents to focus on a recent typical case which best illustrated the school's approach to exclusion.

We did not set out to explore a specific list of factors affecting the use of exclusion. These factors emerged from detailed analysis of interviews.

Clearly the factors which emerged are not statistically robust in the way of large-scale surveys. The emergence of patterns of perceptions and clear contrasts across twelve different schools in different parts of the country suggests, however, that our findings are something more than the idiosyncratic experiences of individual schools. They help to explain how aspects of a school's ethos impinge directly on exclusion rates by understanding the beliefs and ideas which underpin school practices. As in all case study research, however, it is for the reader to gauge the validity of the findings by reflecting on their resonance with the reader's own experience of schools.

Beliefs about schools, teaching and pupils

Understanding exclusion begins with an exploration of staff views about the purposes of the school, the role of the teacher and who counts as an acceptable pupil. This may seem hopelessly abstract and impractical to those engaged in the hurly burly of school life but as our studies of schools with contrasting exclusion rates showed, the more narrowly these questions were answered, the higher the exclusion rate. Schools which saw their main purpose as equipping pupils with good academic qualifications, saw teaching as primarily concerned with subject specific knowledge, and acceptable pupils as those who were well behaved, well motivated and from a home which supported the school, tended to have higher rates of exclusion than those which took a broader view of these matters. This is common sense. The more one specifies and delimits the nature of an organisation and its members, the greater the scope for excluding those who do not conform. We can all think of clubs which effectively restrict membership by specifying entry requirements which are difficult to meet and have adherence to codes of conduct as a condition of membership. Schools are different from clubs in many ways, not least in the fact that most young people aged 5–16 have to attend, have very little say in membership rules and regulations and can have their life chances adversely affected if they break the rules. Let us look more closely at the ways in which beliefs, particularly those held by the senior staff in the school, affected exclusion.

The studies of school effectiveness and of school discipline mentioned above ask rather different questions about schools, employ different approaches to collecting and analysing data and operate within different theoretical frameworks. Yet they are remarkably complementary in identifying particular aspects of school ethos as powerful influences on school outcomes, whether these be the academic attainment of pupils or success in handling pupils' troublesome behaviour. These aspects of school ethos are summarised in Table 4.1 (see page 61).

Leadership, particularly that of the headteacher, has been identified as a key influence on school effectiveness in general and on school discipline in particular. In our study the beliefs of headteachers* were associated with their practices regarding exclusion.

In low excluding schools headteachers believed that it was the job of the school to educate all pupils, not just the well motivated and well behaved. The following quotation is typical although it came from a newly appointed headteacher to a high excluding school.

> I think it is a moral thing, that you've got to say that those youngsters should be in education and it's education for all. It's not just education for the few that come in and don't cause us any problems.
>
> (Headteacher, Lubnaig Secondary School)

---

* We use headteachers as a convenient shorthand for a sample that included headteachers, deputies and assistant headteachers.

Her beliefs were translated into action by changing the system used to exclude pupils so that all exclusions had to be personally authorised by her. She saw it as a major challenge for the school to adopt inclusive values and she was well aware of the management task ahead in terms of persuading her colleagues of the need for such an approach. Headteachers' beliefs in minimising exclusion were reflected in practices which sought to value staff and pupil views while at the same time setting the tone about what the school stood for. The same headteacher continued:

> For many [staff who are nearing retirement] their heyday was in the time when the belt [strap] was about and that was the answer ... and many of them haven't moved out of that mind set. So it's hard for them and for me.
>
> (Headteacher, Lubnaig Secondary School)

Furthermore, headteachers of inclusive schools saw it as a collective responsibility for the staff to motivate pupils, to make learning fun and to make pupils feel valued, as the following quotation makes clear:

> That's my alternative to exclusions – crazy sports, novelty afternoons, being silly. You're constantly changing things with the kids. It's always keeping them on their toes so they'll enjoy what is happening and want to come to school. They like it. School is fun. It's enjoyable. They know the staff like them and want to be with them and the staff are very good at this.
>
> (Headteacher, Menteith Primary School)

They also saw it as their job to support staff by direct action if a youngster was causing problems in the classroom. Thus establishing an inclusive ethos was not only about beliefs and actions to support pupils and to promote positive and enjoyable learning experiences, it meant real practical support for teaching staff when trouble happened.

> The [headteacher and depute headteacher] are brilliant in supporting staff. Anytime you need a break you can send a kid to them and say 'Help! Take [him] off my hands. I'm cracking up.' ... And they will look after [him] to give you a break. It's great, it's a real wee safety net.
>
> (Teacher, Menteith Primary School)

In brief, headteachers of inclusive schools saw it as a responsibility to educate all pupils, to nurture social as well as academic achievements, to stimulate pupil motivation and enjoyment in learning and personally to offer practical support and help to teachers under strain from troublesome pupils. Their management style was consultative but they were clear that it was their responsibility to set the tone.

In contrast headteachers in schools with high exclusion rates tended to specify the school's responsibility in terms of promoting the academic attainment of their pupils, to see pupils causing trouble not being the school's responsibility and to have rather hierarchical line management structures. So, for example, instead of schools having a responsibility to educate all pupils, their responsibility was to educate only those pupils who came willing and ready to learn what the school had to offer.

> I would love not to suspend [i.e. exclude] pupils but and this is a statement from the school – I do not care if in a month I suspend 100 or I suspend none, as long as, at the end of the month, a quality education has been delivered to pupils who come through the gates wishing to learn.
>
> (Acting Headteacher, Tummel Secondary School)

The policy dilemmas for teachers and others in dealing with the needs both of troublesome pupils and with the generality of pupils are considered in Chapter 3. For the moment the point to make is that a headteacher who holds a view like that expressed above is clearly delimiting the school's responsibility. Those excluded are those who do not share the school's highly focused concern with learning and being ready to learn is a *sine qua non* of inclusion in that particular school. The school is accepting neither responsibility for young people who are unready to learn nor the need to change its practices. The school has something to offer and if pupils do not want to take advantage of this, there is no place for them in the school. It is easy to see that a school leader espousing such a set of beliefs will encourage the use of exclusion.

'Worthy or unworthy' of help?

It is also noteworthy that teachers in all schools characterised pupils in trouble as being worthy or unworthy of help. Such characterisation included:

- 'nice' versus 'bad' pupils
- pupils 'whose parents bother' versus pupils 'whose parents don't bother'
- those who 'accept the system' versus those who 'reject the system'
- those with a 'social sense' versus those who are 'egocentric'

- younger pupils (up to age 13–14 – still malleable) versus older pupils
- emotional problems (worthy) versus behavioural problems (unworthy).

The list is taken from one school, illustrating different ways in which certain pupil types were written off as not worthy of the school's attention or care, a tendency also evident in the literature on social, emotional and behavioural difficulties, referred to in Chapter 3. Similar examples were mentioned in other schools. It was striking, however, that schools with higher rates of exclusion identified more categories of unworthy pupils than the lower excluding schools.

It is important to note that within all schools there were tensions and contradictions in terms of prevailing beliefs about the nature of teaching and the role of pupils. Not all staff showed the same view of where the boundaries ought to lie and resistant cultures were in evidence. Thus in schools where dominant beliefs tended towards inclusion, there were staff who resented this. Some teachers in such schools would sometimes challenge the headteacher's loyalty to themselves as professionals by giving examples of occasions when they had been unsupported or treated unsympathetically in the face of a discipline problem and the headteacher had refused to exclude a pupil. Likewise in schools which were readier to exclude, some staff believed the approach was wrong and resisted referring pupils with troublesome behaviour to senior management. This was more apparent in large secondary schools where subject departments could provide a natural locus for alternative points of view. It was less in evidence in primaries where open resistance to dominant beliefs would be more conspicuous among a staff of say 10–15. Although senior management, therefore, defined the key assumptions under which the school used exclusions, individual teachers who did not share these assumptions could also influence exclusion. This suggests that headteachers who wish to reduce the use of exclusion need to persuade almost all staff of the rationale for and benefits of such a policy, if it is to be successful.

The curriculum on offer

A key part of a school's ethos concerns curriculum provision and organisation. For example, organising pupils by ability groups or by setting and streaming is seen by many commentators as having harmful unintended consequences (Sukhandan and Lee, 1998). 'They point out that, when students are divided on the basis of academic criteria,

they also tend to be segregated by social and academic characteristics' (Gamoran *et al.*, 1995:688). This can send messages about who is
valued in the school and about what counts as really useful learning.
If young people perceive that they cannot be successful academic
learners, anxiety and insecurity can result which in turn leads on to
disruptive and avoidance tactics to cover for fear of failure. (see
Goleman, 1996:234–237 for an overview.)

There was a general consensus in the secondary schools studied
that learning difficulties, particularly difficulties in reading and
writing, lay at the root of many behaviour problems. (Chapter 1 gives
a pupil view of this.) Staff saw many of the 14–16-year-olds who were
excluded as lacking motivation to learn, as seeing no purpose in
school work and schools as 'being not for the likes of us'. Although
schools reported similar concerns with the curriculum (namely as
being overly academic, the demands of portfolios of work for
Standard Grade examinations requiring regular and consistent effort
on the part of pupils, and the pressures to present all pupils for 7–8
Standard Grades regardless of their ability to cope) they varied
markedly in their approach to tackling these concerns.

The lower excluding schools recognised the importance of offering
all pupils the opportunity to experience success and acceptance as
part of the school community. They did this in many different ways.
For example, through the informal curriculum of clubs and societies,
developing and valuing participation in drama, music and art through
exhibitions, school shows and concerts, pupils were given opportunities to demonstrate creativity, organisational skills, and talents in
public relations. These schools too also valued personal and social
development slots in the curriculum which were regularly timetabled
and had an agreed syllabus. Low excluding schools tended to exper-
iment with the curriculum on offer, being flexible in the number of
subjects pupils were expected to study and using learning support as
a resource for mainstream staff to consult about differentiating curriculum materials. In contrast, high excluding schools tended to have
few out-of-school activities, stressed their core business of teaching
the academic curriculum and expected learning support teachers to
extract pupils experiencing difficulties from the mainstream classroom.

School relations with the outside world

In this section we look briefly at relations between school and home
and between school and 'external professionals' such as educational

psychologists and social workers as a way of revealing how school ethos can influence exclusion.

All the primary and secondary schools studied believed that it was crucial for parents to support the school in terms of its behaviour and discipline policy. Parental support was important both in avoiding exclusion in the first place, through working with the school to avoid the escalation of trouble, and if that failed, in making an exclusion effective in changing behaviour. As one senior manager said:

> One of the most crucial things in exclusion . . . in terms of whether it is a success or not, or whether it is a deterrent or not . . . is the parental reaction and the extent of parental support.
>
> (Depute headteacher, Ness Secondary School)

This view was not disputed; what did vary between the schools was the degree to which parental support was actively sought, as opposed to being simply expected. Broadly speaking, schools with lower exclusion levels had key staff who worked hard to build a two-way relationship with the parents of children in trouble. These staff were typically designated behaviour support staff and senior managers. Strategies used included inviting parents to meetings where their child's difficulties were the focus of a problem-solving effort by all present. Such meetings were seen as a useful way of breaking down stereotypes on both sides. Although resource intensive in terms of staff and time, such meetings could build up an atmosphere of mutual trust as the following extract from a parent interview makes clear.

> I was totally against them [school] but as time goes on, I realised it's not really their fault and you've got to try and work together and that's what we've done. You're trying to stick up for your children, but we do work well together now. I think that's why [the teacher] puts up with what she does from Matthew, because we've given each other support throughout it all. Otherwise, I think he would have been out of school a long time ago.
>
> (Mrs P., Katrin Primary parent)

All the parents interviewed saw school as worthwhile and even where there were severe behavioural problems had not given up on their children and wanted them to succeed. Thus any perceived failure on the part of school could assume the scale of a major deliberate omission. Feelings of stress and anger were common, particularly from mothers. They 'felt mad', 'felt I could just scream', 'didn't know where to turn' and 'felt at the end of my tether'. These feelings are reported from other small-scale studies involving parents of excluded children (Parsons,

1996a; Cohen *et al.*,1994), and reported more extensively in Chapter 1.

In these circumstances it is hardly surprising that misunderstandings occur, breakdowns in communication happen and all kinds of motives are attributed to one side by the other. Teachers feel stressed too. Yet low excluding schools were characterised by a commitment to working with parents, being less judgemental about their circumstances and by seeing two-way communication between home and school as really important. High excluding schools tended to expect parents' unquestioning support and to condemn them if this was not immediately apparent.

A similar picture was evident in contrasting approaches to working with external professionals. Where teachers saw themselves as responsible for teaching only the well behaved and ready to learn, external professionals tended to be seen as there to 'cure' disaffected pupils who would then return to mainstream classes or, where this was possible, to facilitate out-of-school placement. Where teachers saw themselves as responsible for teaching all children, these external professionals were viewed as partners in the joint task of helping to solve the problems evinced by the pupils. Rather than offering particular examples of this approach in action, we list, on the basis of our data, a number of factors which increased the likelihood of successful joint working. These were that external professionals should be involved:

- early, preferably before the situation reached exclusion stage (indeed, one interviewee felt that the official procedures on exclusion should be slowed down so that appropriate support from, for example, Social Work, had to be tried first)
- appropriately, that is, depending on the nature of the underlying problem and not automatically regardless of the underlying problem
- as partners with the school and, if possible, with the parents
- with an agreed purpose and with realistic aims
- for the shortest effective time relative to the agreed aims.

Of course, it is much easier to set out such factors than to put them into practice in a context of competition for declining resources, increasing workloads on all professionals, and very different professional ideologies. Yet we were given examples of cases of real pupils where successful intervention carrying all these hallmarks took place. Crucially, this resulted from good personal relations between the key school contact, often a support centre teacher (in secondary) or the headteacher (in primary), and the external professional(s) involved.

Such relationships did not happen by chance, but required work over time from all involved. This work was facilitated by open or 'sharing' professional ideologies. We explore work with outside agencies as an alternative to exclusion in Chapter 5. For the moment we wish to emphasise that a school's ethos influences relations with outside agencies and so its predisposition to exclude children.

Decision making about exclusion

The way in which systems of school discipline and of pastoral support operate can be seen as embodying the ethos of the school. In the case study schools there was a clear association between dominant beliefs about the purposes of the school, the teacher's role and the acceptable pupil on the one hand and the systems for pupil discipline and welfare on the other. High excluding schools tended to have hierarchical decision making about exclusions through progressively more senior staff culminating in the headteacher. Lower excluding schools tended to have a network of people involved in decision making. This network usually consisted of a pastoral care teacher, behaviour support staff and senior management. The crucial systems level factor was the degree of separation between discipline referral systems on the one hand and pastoral care systems on the other. The more divorced they were, in terms of personnel and structures, the more likely was exclusion. This factor affected the use of exclusion even in the lower excluding schools. An educational psychologist working with one such school drew attention to this:

> I certainly perceive at times the Joint Assessment Team [a multi-agency team] and the pastoral system working in one way and the senior management team and the discipline system working completely [in another] way. ... We are discussing who should be involved [in supporting children and] what kind of support should be in place and the discipline system seems to be working to get them out. ... It seems to me that the senior management and the discipline system in exclusions is more powerful in that dichotomy.
> (Educational psychologist, Tay Secondary School)

Joint Assessment Teams consist of a range of individuals likely to know of, or be involved in a professional capacity with, pupils at risk of exclusion. They would usually comprise a senior member of school management, pastoral and/or behaviour support staff, educational psychologist, social worker and sometimes a doctor as well as the parent of the pupil at risk. These teams tended to discuss extreme cases. Where discipline and pastoral care systems were divorced, less extreme cases would typically be handled through discipline structures and short multiple exclusions could result.

Thus the role and function of pastoral care staff, behaviour support staff and learning support staff in schools could influence exclusion rates. Higher excluding schools tended to divorce pastoral care and discipline structures and so guidance staff were not involved in decisions about exclusion. Lower excluding schools in contrast tended to see pastoral care staff as an important source of information about pupils and their staff were involved in decision making about exclusion. Both high and low excluding schools had behaviour support staff but varied in the way they used them. Some lower excluding schools had encouraged collaboration between learning support and behaviour support staff to provide professional support to teachers in mainstream classes to minimise the risk of troublesome behaviour arising from learning difficulties. These specialist staff were also important sources of information in any decisions about exclusion. Behaviour support staff in higher excluding schools tended to be used mainly in units or bases and not to be involved in decision making about exclusion.

Discipline systems which were escalatory, made the road to exclusion very easy. As a social worker said of Lubnaig School:

> Youngsters who are disillusioned with school . . . and basically want to be out of it – then all they have to do is swear at a senior member of staff. It's easy [to be excluded]. I could do it! . . . Discipline is handled by one member of the senior management team. They hand out punishment exercises and if [the youngsters] don't do them so many times, they end up getting detention. . . . If they don't go to detention they get excluded. These things happen without anyone knowing about them.

It was clear though that even such escalatory systems were open to negotiation, depending on the pupil concerned and the fuss likely to be made by the parent. One headteacher recounted a case where an articulate and contrite pupil, backed up by a supportive mother, was able to negotiate his way out of a decision to exclude him. This small example reveals that exclusion is not inevitable in such systems. The pupil and parent need to demonstrate adherence to the same values as the senior staff, and repentance, to avoid exclusion taking place. Furthermore it reveals something of the complexity of school practices regarding exclusion and the difficulty in unambiguously classifying decision-making structures.

Table 4.1. School ethos and exclusion

Encouraged exclusion ◄──────────────► Discouraged exclusion	
Beliefs about school, teaching and pupils	
Narrow definition of teacher's job, focused on subject knowledge, exam results	Wide remit, including personal and social development of pupils, as well as exam results
Academic goals prominent	Social and academic goals
Acceptable pupils were those who arrived willing to learn, and came from supportive homes	Acceptance of a wide range of pupils, including those with learning and other difficulties
The curriculum	
Academic curriculum, pressure on pupils, lack of differentiation	Curriculum flexible and differentiated
Personal and social development curriculum lacks status	Personal and social development curriculum highly valued
Potential of informal curriculum for motivating less academic pupils not realised	Informal curriculum, lively and covering a wide range of activities, such as sport, drama, art, working in the local community
Relations with parents	
Parents expected unquestioningly to support the school	Time and effort spent involving parents in decision making about their children
Decision making about exclusion	
Hierarchical decision making separating pastoral support staff from those with responsibility for maintaining discipline	Decisions informed by a network of staff with a range of perspectives on the pupil
Tariff systems leading to automatic exclusion	Flexible system, behaviour evaluated in context
Pastoral support staff expected to meet needs of all pupils	Pastoral support staff an information source on decisions
Learning/behaviour support expected to remove troublesome pupils and solve problems	Learning/behaviour support a source of support and ideas for mainstream staff

A summary of the way school ethos affects exclusion

School ethos is hard to grasp because it pervades so many aspects of school life, routines and rituals that we take for granted. This chapter illustrated ways in which ethos, the underpinning beliefs and practices of schools, can encourage or discourage the use of exclusion. The summary below is also intended as a checklist of the ethos in your school. Changing a school's ethos is difficult but it can be done. You need to start, though, from an understanding of where the school is and where collectively it wants to be.

Three strategies for developing a positive ethos

There is a vast literature on bringing about change in schools and it is not our intention to add to it. Indeed change is often seen as so complex and involving so many elements that a certain paralysis by analysis can set in. In this section we present three broad strategies used by a number of schools to tackle low level, persistent indiscipline. These strategies are at whole-school level and were introduced in response to particular discipline problems. Schools have found, however, that they have had a beneficial effect on their ethos. In particular, pupils feel valued and so are less likely to cause trouble; cynical school staff have their beliefs challenged about the immutability of difficult behaviour; and, in general, schools have become more pleasant places in which to work.

The strategies outlined below are by no means a panacea for tackling exclusion. Schools can have a positive ethos and still encounter young people with serious social, emotional and behavioural difficulties. Nevertheless many short-term, temporary exclusions are for relatively trivial offences such as insolence or refusal to obey rules. Furthermore sometimes arguments and fights among pupils at break or lunchtime spill over into the classroom and so strategies which encourage constructive use of these times, for instance, can be helpful. The strategies reported here have not been subject to rigorous external evaluation. Rather they are accounts by teachers of real attempts to improve school discipline and thereby their ethos (Munn, 1999). The three strategies are:

- praise and reward systems
- structuring breaks and lunchtimes
- pupil participation in decision making.

Praise and reward systems

Most of us are not as positive as we think we are. Smith (1998) quotes a recent UK study based on observations of children at home and in school, which showed that on an average day they received 460 negative or critical comments compared with 75 positive or supportive comments. Mortimore *et al.* (1988) in their study of 50 London junior schools found that teachers spent less than one per cent of their time giving praise. Schools seem to be much more likely to specify sanctions and punishments for poor behaviour than to recognise and reward good behaviour. Indeed the spur to one secondary school deciding to adopt a positive approach to discipline was the realisation that its system of sanctions 'had one simple failing, it doesn't have any effect' (Sinclair, 1999:40). Indeed instances of poor behaviour and the number of exclusions were rising and although some staff favoured more and more severe sanctions, others wanted a more fundamental review of the whole issue. A small working group was set up which surveyed staff views, reviewed the literature on school discipline, and visited other schools experimenting with positive approaches. After a great deal of consultation with staff and parents of intending first year pupils a system of praise cards was developed. These led to successively more impressive certificates, the most prestigious of which is presented by the headteacher. The idea of 'catching pupils getting it right' is now becoming established across the school and praise certificates are 'cool' for 14–16-year-olds as well as younger pupils. Alongside the praise system a clear system of dealing with misbehaviour has been established with the highest level sanction being that the pupil is sent to a partner teacher's room and the parents invited to come to the school. The headteacher reports that such removals average 4–6 on a bad day with none on a good day. Under the previous system up to 30 pupils could be on report in one day.

Praise systems are by no means a panacea and have to be introduced thoughtfully. They are most commonly associated with Assertive Discipline systems associated with Canter and Canter (1992). Essentially this approach rests on three components: i) make your requirements clear (publish clear, unambiguous rules); ii) give continuous positive feedback when pupils are successfully meeting your requirements; iii) publish a hierarchy of mild but irksome sanctions for rule breaking. This package has been available in the United Kingdom since the early 1990s and has received a largely positive press although debates about its underlying authoritarian tone and philosophy have been raging in academic journals. (see e.g. Swinson and Melling, 1995; Robinson and Maines, 1994a, 1994b, 1995). No system to be applied in a complex institution such as a school can be used 'off the shelf'. Most of the schools involved in writing about the introduction and use of their systems highlight the following steps:

- surveys of staff views
- research on positive systems including visits to schools operating these
- the use of an external consultant/adviser to get the ball rolling
- the need to promote consistency in the use of both praise and sanctions
- devising a system that is easy and straightforward to operate
- keeping the system under review to sustain motivation of staff and students
- the need to customise a system to a school's particular circumstances.

Nevertheless such systems involve teachers in examining their normal practice and as such can be a good starting point for further explorations of a school's ethos. Introduced without careful consultation, monitoring and review, such systems can quickly degenerate into the overuse of sanctions or meaningless recognition of commonplace behaviour. Smith (1998) highlights the need for praise to be for specific and meaningful achievements and for teachers to be aware that they can be used as a means of inducing people to conform, of manipulating and controlling people. 'Overuse of praise may limit the opportunity for students to develop their own decision-making ability and can reduce their ability to self-evaluate' (Smith, 1998:5). This is why schools need to spend time working out the general criteria for praise points and to consider carefully what counts as a reward. Rewards such as free time out of school or coming to school having had a lie-in which devalue the notion of learning do not seem appropriate. The benefit of such systems is that they encourage teachers to reflect on the school's influence on pupil behaviour. The disadvantage is that they can be used as a quick fix without serious reflection on the multiple explanations for troubled behaviour and reinforce stereotypical power relations between pupil and teacher, hardly conducive to pupil self-discipline and critical autonomy.

Breaks and lunchtimes

The importance of play and social interaction is generally recognised in social-cognitive development (see Pellegrini and Smith, 1993 for a review). Tizard *et al.* (1988) showed on the basis of observations of

7-year-olds in 33 inner London schools that 28 per cent of the school day was spent at break time and lunch. However, when break time is being considered in schools it tends to be seen as a problem (Blatchford and Sumpner, 1998). This view was influenced not only by individual violent acts, such as the murder of a British Asian boy in a Manchester secondary school leading to a public enquiry (Macdonald, 1989), but also the long lunch break was highlighted by the Elton Committee (DES, 1989) as 'the single biggest behaviour-related problem that [staff] face'.

The surveys for the Elton Committee and beyond report two-thirds or more of secondary teachers encountering physical aggression among pupils at least once a week around the school; over 77 per cent of Scottish primary teachers and 86 per cent of their English colleagues reported this. Blatchford and Sumpner (1998) report that in their large-scale survey of break time, examining the current situation and changes over the past five years, there was a tendency at primary level for teachers to consider that break time had improved, but at secondary level to feel behaviour had stayed the same. In one in four schools, at both primary and secondary, the view was that behaviour at break time had declined. (It should be noted that the survey was completed by one person on behalf of the school, usually the headteacher.)

Boulton (1993a) interviewed 110 pupils aged 8 and 11 about why children in general and the respondents in particular fought with fellow pupils in the playground. Some 51 per cent of children reported having had at least one aggressive fight during the previous year. The most common reasons for fighting were retaliations to teasing, retaliation to unprovoked assault, disagreement over aspects of a game, dislike of a child and to settle dominance disputes. This study was followed by others using i) direct observation and ii) *in situ* interviews combined with observation. Aggressive retaliation to teasing and aggressive retaliation to accidental hurt were two of the main sources of fighting but to an adult observer, some 43 per cent of observed fights among younger pupils had no obvious immediate cause (Boulton, 1993b). The importance of teasing in provoking a response by fighting was also a feature of the data collected by Mooney *et al.* (1991) in a follow-up study of 11-year-old children first interviewed at age 7. Name calling can also provoke fighting and thus be a reason for exclusion (CRE, 1996; Cohen *et al.*, 1994).

Many schools are developing their grounds both as a source of education about the environment and as a way of promoting positive discipline. Activities for discipline include, in primary schools, the recruiting of playground helpers from among older pupils who have to apply for the post and be interviewed, training for these helpers and for adult playground supervisors, the designation of particular areas for quiet activities, the provision of a range of equipment, the establishing of a rota for particular games. Again as in the introduction of praise and reward systems, consulting staff, parents and pupils about the nature of problems in the playground and ways of overcoming these features in successful initiatives. In secondary and primary schools buddy systems have been introduced whereby younger children have older buddies to help them become used to a new school environment and be a source of help in times of trouble. Such systems, of course, need careful selection and training of buddies but they are ways of signalling that maintaining a safe and secure environment is the responsibility of all members of the school community, not just the teachers.

Pupil participation in decision making

Involving pupils in decision making about matters which affect them can help establish a sense of fairness and justice about school rules, sanctions and rewards. An opportunity at classroom level to debate the need for rules, for example, increases the likelihood that they will be seen as reasonable and thus be obeyed. Similarly a pupil council with real decision-making powers and a budget can help promote a positive ethos by recognising that pupils have legitimate concerns about and abilities to solve problems around break times, lavatories, the library, school food and the like, which loom large in their life and about which teachers may be unaware. Naturally the establishment of class and school councils needs care and constitutions need to be drawn up, representatives elected and the like. This is an approach which can promote understanding of active citizenship as well as a positive ethos.

The benefits of pupil participation in the negotiation of rules, rewards and sanctions emerge from a number of studies. Pritchard and Barker (1996) describe the beneficial effects of negotiating a class contract with 11–16-year-olds when they taught at the British Institute in Bilbao, Spain. They highlight the anticipation of problems and the sense of ownership such a negotiation can bring. Langford *et al.* (1994) report two studies among a total of 117 senior secondary school students in Australia highlighting the recognition by the majority of the need for rules. They conclude that it is possible to reach apparent agreement with most students about rules. Similarly Munn *et al.* (1992a) report pupils' dissatisfaction with and hence disruption caused by rules whose rationale is obscure or unfair. Garner (1992) advocates involving 'disruptive' students in the creation and sustaining of school discipline structures, while John and Osborn (1992), from the perspective of promoting citizenship and democratic values, argue for pupil involvement in decision making.

One of the case study schools involved in our research had a new headteacher who was actively trying to turn around an established culture of high exclusions. In the following extract from an interview with her, she describes the use of pupil participation in decision making as one important strand of this process and explains how it went hand in hand with a related strategy involving more staff in decision making.

Headteacher: The ethos was very disciplinarian – no negotiation, no backing down, that type of thing. It was very much a black and white situation and something that I'm really trying to change within the school.

Interviewer: Do you have any thoughts on how you might approach that?

Headteacher: The youngsters have a very negative image of themselves and a very negative image of the school itself. I interviewed all the staff when I arrived and a fair number of pupils. The pupils' perception is that it is a 'mingin' school' [laughs]. [Usually 'minging' means dirty but here it means 'unpleasant'.] They really do have a very low self-image so [I am] actually trying to involve them (and involve the staff) in decision making and giving them a wee bit of power within the school to see what they can actually do with it.

The staff spent a whole morning on a recent in-service day telling me what they wanted from the school and I did a similar thing with pupils one afternoon. We stopped all classes and the pupils worked in groups telling me what they wanted from the school. So we're moving forwards and that improves how they feel about things and how things operate. . . . . The youngsters have chosen a colour for a sweatshirt – they've never had a [school] sweatshirt before. It just makes them feel a wee bit better about themselves, so things should improve within the school and, hopefully, that will be able to help the discipline within the school and things like that.

(Headteacher, Lubnaig Secondary School)

The Scottish Schools Ethos Network

The importance of school ethos for a number of school outcomes led to the development in Scotland of 'ethos indicators' for primary and secondary schools. The indicators grew out of research and development work funded by the Scottish Office which identified key aspects of ethos for schools and suggested ways in which schools might evaluate their ethos and identify aspects for improvement (SOED, 1992a, 1992b). The list contained many items and has now been subsumed in a school self-evaluation handbook *How Good is Our School?* (SOEID, 1996.) Schools are therefore being encouraged to evaluate their ethos and are being given the tools to do so. Underpinning this approach is a belief that 'the most effective way of improving the quality of education for individual pupils is to expect schools to take responsibility for their own quality assurance by evaluating their performance and making the necessary changes' (HM Inspectors of Schools, 1996). This belief means that national standards in Scotland are monitored in a variety of ways against key criteria developed by HMI. A school's ethos is an important area for self evaluation.

The ethos network grew out of schools' attempts to evaluate their ethos and to promote positive changes. The network is managed by a small core of staff at the University of Edinburgh. With well over 1,000 members the network provides a forum in which schools can share ideas and experiences through newsletters, case studies, seminars and conferences. A membership database means that schools can make direct links with others working on similar features of their ethos. Discipline is an important aspect of ethos and the Scottish Office funded a separate programme involving 60 schools in promoting positive discipline.

The point to emphasise is that schools need practical support in evaluating and developing their ethos. A national framework provides one kind of support but having direct access to the warts and all experience of other schools is invaluable in helping schools envisage how they might promote a positive ethos. The network stresses the importance of a collective understanding of ethos by seeking the views of pupils, parents, support staff and teaching staff of how they experience aspects of school life. This collective understanding needs to be accompanied by a collective commitment to change practices which are experienced as demeaning for members of the school community. This is easy to say, of course, much harder to put into practice.

Conclusion

The early part of the chapter illustrates ways in which a school's ethos can encourage or restrain the exclusion of pupils. We hope it will convince teachers and others involved in education that ethos is a key feature in understanding why schools with similar pupils vary in the use they make of exclusion. We also hope it will encourage local groups of schools to set up their own networking arrangements to share experiences and ideas. Ethos is a slippery concept, embodying beliefs and practices which schools take for granted about the way they operate. Thus the more schools are able to share with others what they do and why they do it when it comes to exclusion, the more they will be able to examine the rationale for and the reasonableness of their practices.

Table 4.1 summarises key dimensions of ethos which, on the basis of case studies of contrasting schools, emerged as important in explaining high and low exclusion rates. These key dimensions were:

- beliefs about the purposes of schools, teaching and the nature of pupils
- the curriculum on offer, and particularly the opportunities for pupils to experience successful learning and a sense of achievement
- school relations with the outside world
- decision-making structures for exclusion.

Clearly beliefs about teaching and children are the most difficult to change. The chapter gave examples of particular strategies such as the sensitive use of praise and reward systems, the imaginative use of breaks and lunchtimes and pupil involvement in decision-making which can help challenge beliefs about the school's lack of ability to promote good behaviour. None of these strategies is a panacea, of course, and good behaviour has to be continually encouraged through a variety of approaches. Specific practices to counter exclusion are discussed in Chapter 5. This chapter has stressed the importance of such practices being embedded in a school ethos which discourages exclusion.

5

Sanctions and Support: School Responses to 'Challenging' Behaviour

> You should not be going from containment to crisis. There should be lots of different strategies ... No child should go from nothing to disaster.
>
> (Kinder *et al.*, 1999a:32)

This chapter is in two main parts reflecting rather different ways of thinking about alternatives to exclusion. The first part examines alternative *sanctions* to that of exclusion, a different way of punishing challenging behaviour which would otherwise have led to an exclusion. The second part explores approaches which help to *minimise challenging behaviour* which would otherwise lead to exclusion. A theme running through this chapter is the importance of school ethos (see Chapter 4) for both the readiness to try alternatives to exclusion and the purposes of these alternatives. The same alternative, for example a child being withdrawn from a particular class, might be seen as a sanction in one school or as a supportive way of helping the child cope in another school. The chapter reports strategies used in the schools involved in our exclusions research and places these in the context of other research findings.

Many factors in addition to school ethos have to be taken into account in understanding the use of alternatives to exclusion. These include the age and stage of the child, the kind of behaviour in question, the history of the child's behaviour in school, family circumstances, the resources available to the school and in the local authority as well as the skills, knowledge and beliefs of teachers. This chapter then does not set out a checklist of 'what works' as alternatives to exclusion. Such a list would be naïve and an underestimation of the complexity of circumstances in which decisions to exclude are undertaken. Furthermore, research on effectiveness of particular alternatives

70

is usually small scale and descriptive of particular schools, useful in itself but providing no statistical basis for generalisation. There is also the conceptual difficulty of clarifying what counts as effective – an issue explored in greater depth in Chapter 7. Such conceptualisations can range from the behaviour desisting to a pupil's academic attainment and/or active participation in school life. Rather the chapter provides examples of alternatives to exclusion used by real schools. Its starting point is that of the need to understand practice which reduces exclusion so that such practice can be shared, debated and, where appropriate, tried out. As Chapter 4 indicated, the use of particular strategies can be influential in changing the beliefs of teachers and others about schools' influences on behaviour.

Sanctions

Schools have a wide range of sanctions open to them as responses to undesirable behaviour apart from exclusion. These include withdrawal of privileges from the offending pupil, extra work, detention, and a telling off involving parents being present. In our research three particular kinds of sanctions were used which seemed to us to be alternative forms of exclusion in that the pupil was being denied the opportunity to take part in the formal curriculum on offer in the school and so, potentially, the opportunity to learn. These were unofficial sending home, part-time school attendance and internal exclusion. We consider each of these briefly in turn and use them to illustrate the illusions which may be created by the use of statistical targets for schools in respect of reductions in exclusion rates.

Sending home

Many commentators point out the difficulty of obtaining accurate figures about the nature and extent of exclusion in Britain (e.g. Lawrence and Hayden, 1997; Parsons, 1996a, 1999; Imich, 1994; Stirling, 1992; Munn *et al.*, 2000). One of the reasons for this is the widespread use by schools of informal exclusion, sending pupils home without officially recording this as an exclusion on the pupil's record. Our research revealed that such practice was widespread even in schools whose local authorities had explicitly forbidden it. Scottish Office guidance (1998) also draws attention to the illegality of this practice but anecdotal evidence abounds that it continues. Nor is this phenomenon confined to Scotland as research by Gilborn (1998) and others makes clear. Often the use of informal exclusion is perceived as being less serious and therefore a less confrontational way of bringing to parents' attention the degree of their child's misbehaviour in the eyes of the school. It also allows for negotiation between home and school about when such sending home is convenient. It can thus be supportive to parents as the following extract makes clear.

> We've made the agreement that . . . I get home from work at 1.30 and if [my son] has had a bad morning, I just collect him then. [The headteacher] could quite easily suspend [i.e. exclude] him for things he's done in the last few weeks, but she's not because she knows it would interfere with my work . . . There's nobody else to watch [look after] him.
>
> (Mrs P., parent, Katrin Primary School)

Ofsted (1993), however, notes a rather different purpose of informal exclusion, namely persuading parents to withdraw their children from school before a formal exclusion occurs. Presumably schools argue the need for a fresh start on the part of the pupil and the likelihood of a new school place being found if the pupil does not have a formal record of exclusion.

Part-time attendance

Part-time attendance can often be used as part of a package to support children who find it difficult to cope with full-time attendance at a mainstream school. Such a package usually involves alternative provision from a special school or further education college to complement what the mainstream school has to offer. However, part-time attendance used as a sanction was reported by two of the case study schools in the Scottish research. In both of these cases the pupil was permitted to attend school for mornings only and no supplementary provision was made available. In one of these cases, a five-year-old girl was refused permission to attend school in the afternoons over a period of six months. Although the school argued that this was in the child's best interests, her parents and the child herself understood it as a punishment for bad behaviour as the following extract from an interview shows.

> They reckoned that she wasn't ready for full time in school so I let it go for a wee while. Then [she] started getting a bit annoyed about it herself, asking '[Why] am I the only one getting taken out of class at dinner time and not getting to go back?' So I told her that she had to learn to behave herself and things like that. I think myself

that she should have been allowed in a lot earlier than she was.

(Mr R., parent, Katrin Primary School)

Like sending home, this alternative has many of the disadvantages of exclusion but carries no right to legal appeal. (Parents can appeal against formal exclusion.) On the other hand, unlike exclusion, part-time attendance maintains some contact with the school and so access to part of the normal curriculum as well as maintaining limited contact with other children, clearly important for a five-year-old.

Internal exclusion

The most commonly used alternative to exclusion was some form of internal exclusion, or time out of class. (Other names such as isolation, academic remove and class exclusion are sometimes used.) Such internal exclusion could involve the pupils spending part of the day with the headteacher, or exclusion from a particular subject, or from a particular class. The key dimensions of internal exclusion in all its forms were: i) whether it entailed supervision by the class teacher or by another member of staff; and ii) the kind of work, if any, undertaken during this time, as the following example shows:

> So, she was on class exclusion . . . She had to work downstairs. I sent her work downstairs and she worked with the promoted staff, because that gave me time to spend with the other children and get my teaching done.

(Class teacher, Menteith Primary School)

All kinds of variations on these two dimensions are possible as illustrated in Figure 5.1.

Internal exclusion raises a number of issues, particularly where a pupil is spending either a substantial period of each day out of class or is being excluded from one subject area over a long period of time. Arguments against a prolonged use of internal exclusion where no purposive work is being undertaken concern a loss of educational opportunity. This kind of internal exclusion also involved difficulties of reintegration to the regular class or subject area and catching up with missed work. On the positive side, where internal exclusion means that the pupil joins a different class but with a subject specialist and undertakes the same work, it can help. It also sustains a routine of attending school. Clearly much depends on the length of the internal exclusion, on the kind of work being undertaken and on the availability of teaching support. When used frequently it is impossible to ignore the impoverishment of educational experience which

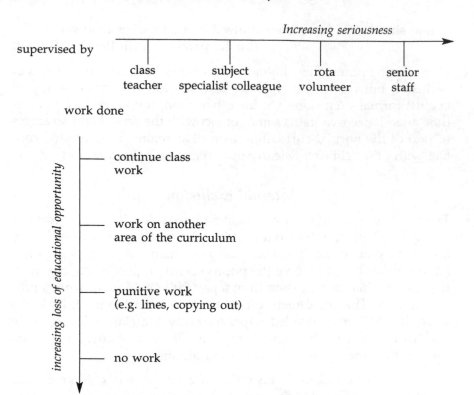

Figure 5.1.   Dimensions of internal exclusion

results as the real case of Matthew, aged eight, exemplifies. Matthew had been excluded in the past and was likely to cause problems where physical activity was concerned. His teacher decided that it was best for the other children in the class if Matthew was excluded from drama, PE and art. His teacher explained:

> if there's a lot of motion or things going on where you can't supervise him all the time, we tend to exclude him [from those activities] and give him more set work. It tends to be quite easy work ... pitched just below his level so he can actually work through [it] and get a sense of achievement from finishing something.

Matthew, who told us that gym was his favourite part of school, perhaps not surprisingly, 'hates' his teacher:

> I hate him. He keeps me in. I am not allowed to choose. I'm not allowed to move around when others are allowed to.

The extreme nature of this case is highlighted by the fact that other members of staff were concerned; as one said:

I think it might be better if [Matthew] was excluded. He would be no worse off at home because he is hardly in the classroom anyway . . . I think he spends about 75 per cent of his time out of class, it's certainly at least 50 per cent. He sits in the corridor. He sits and sits and sits and sits.

In thinking about the advantages and disadvantages of internal rather than external exclusion it is important to bear in mind the spectrum of seriousness illustrated in Figure 5.1. Clearly it is preferable to have to spend five or ten minutes in the corridor to settle down than to be excluded from school. On the other hand, some schools may use internal exclusion to an extreme, as in Matthew's case, or, in a large secondary school, be unaware of the extent to which individual pupils are being internally excluded. The invisible nature of internal exclusion both prevents the possibility of legal redress by parents who may be unaware that it is happening, and prevents the seriousness of the child's problems being brought to the attention of the local education authority. Like informal exclusion, internal exclusion may stem from a belief that it is acting in the child's best interests to avoid official exclusion or because alternative provision is not available. Furthermore the pupil's home circumstances may be such that exclusion would only increase the risk to the pupil.

All kinds of explanations and motives may underlie the use of internal exclusion. Nevertheless a reliance on performance management systems using statistical indicators to chart exclusion rates may conceal poor quality educational provision in schools for pupils in trouble even if fewer pupils are being formally excluded. Schools are not accountable for the time spent by pupils on internal exclusion or for what is offered in the way of teaching to such pupils. This is an issue to which we return in the final chapter. For the moment we can note that Matthew's case was resolved, at least to the school's satisfaction, as he was found a place in a special school. We have no way of knowing how many other 'Matthews' there are in primary schools in Britain and how long they have to wait before they obtain access to a full curriculum.

All of the punitive alternatives to exclusion mentioned above have one common element, namely the removal of the disruptive child from the classroom or school. This was seen by teachers as sharing the same positive characteristics of exclusion itself, it allows other pupils to get on with their work, it gives teachers respite from dealing with a persistently disruptive pupil, makes a public statement about standards of behaviour and has a good effect on the behaviour of other pupils. The use of exclusion, informal, formal or internal, to protect other children was a theme in research on teachers' perceptions of indiscipline in Scotland (Munn *et al.*, 1998). The following views were typical (Johnstone and Munn, 1997:42):

> In general, exclusion has little beneficial effect on the excluded child. However, only someone who had dealt on a daily basis with a severely disruptive, violent child, knows the benefits that even a short-term exclusion can bring to the rest of the class.
>
> (Primary school teacher)

> Exclusion means that the rest of the pupils can get on with their work without being intimidated or constantly disrupted.
>
> (Secondary school teacher)

Teachers report that a 'silent cheer goes up from the silent majority [of pupils] when a disruptive pupil is excluded' and that parents of this silent majority likewise welcome strong action on the part of the school (Cullen *et al.*, 1996). This suggests that if pressure is placed on schools to reduce formal exclusion we can anticipate an increase in informal exclusion and in internal exclusions.

Units and bases

Units and bases may be considered as a bridge between strategies classified as sanctions or support. Many schools have developed special bases or units which may operate as part of a school's system either of sanctions or of support, or sometimes rather uneasily as part of both (Kinder *et al.*, 1995; McNeill, 1996). The failure of both off-site units and segregated on-site units to reintegrate pupils into mainstream school led more recently in the UK to the development of a more flexible model of in-school units where pupils are more rarely placed full time (Gray and Noakes, 1993; Rennie, 1993; Barrow, 1995; Farrell and Tsakalidou, 1999). Sometimes such units are staffed by teachers who have specialist skills developed in more segregated settings. Units may be seen as offering the opportunity for pupils to have respite and support in a small group while still having access to mainstream curricula. Sometimes in the early years withdrawal places are called nurture groups (Bennathan and Boxall, 1996).

Units to which pupils are referred as punishment (described as sin-bins in the dissent to the Scottish Pack report (SED, 1977) in which the majority recommended the setting up of units) are sometimes used as the last resort before exclusion (Kinder *et al.*, 1995). In this kind of unit pupils are usually supervised, sometimes by a rota of class or subject teachers, while continuing with their class work. In units or bases with a broader supportive role the staff may be full-time with a remit both to support individual pupils and to develop wider school support systems. Holland and Homerton (1994) list the advantages and disadvantages of this approach, which encourages the development of all school staff, particularly pastoral care staff and group tutors. They recognise that with more focused work in a pupils' support base there can be help for the most difficult pupils, a breathing space for class teachers, effective co-ordination of external agencies, a calm environment and flexibility, but that the mainstream teachers are more likely to disown the problem, there is less support for most pupils and the skills stay with a few people who are less likely to provide an early response to difficulty. Sinclair Taylor, who argues for the value of special units, also found special unit pupils to be socially marginalised (Sinclair Taylor, 1995).

The development of behaviour support services in schools is associated in much of the literature with a move away from the use of units, particularly off-site units. This move reflects a critical view of alternative educational provision, in particular of limited curricula and the very low rate of reintegration into mainstream (McLean and Brown, 1992; Gray and Noakes, 1993; Rennie, 1993; Barrow, 1995, 1996; McNeill, 1996; Cullen and Lloyd, 1997). Behaviour support services often emphasise co-operative working with teachers to support or change their classroom management. Sometimes this kind of consultancy role is undertaken by educational psychologists or by designated behaviour support teachers who may be permanently on the staff of a school or peripatetic, the latter often serving several primary schools.

The difficulties of effective joint working are well known in the literature concerning the work of learning support staff. One research project found the following conditions to be necessary for effective joint working between learning support and subject staff in secondary schools:

- the members of staff concerned need time to get to know each other, build up trust, and see their relationship as evolving rather than set in stone;
- non-contact time needs to be available for the learning support teacher and the mainstream teacher to plan lessons together;
- learning support staff need to be reasonably confident about their knowledge of the subject to be taught;
- subject staff recognise the distinctive skills and knowledge of the learning support staff.

(Munn, 1994)

It seems likely that these would also be effective conditions for the consultancy/support relationship implied in behaviour support. There is very little research on effective behaviour support systems and what there is is not widely disseminated (Barrow, 1996; Miller, 1994). There is also little written on the question of appropriate training and professional development of behaviour support staff.

Kinder *et al.* (1995:29) identified as a key issue in the effectiveness of behaviour support staff the extent to which the 'objectives and procedures of behaviour related roles were accepted and understood by staff and the central role which senior managers played in their successful integration'.

The role of classroom assistants

There has been a recent increase in the use of classroom auxiliaries or assistants to support troublesome pupils. Some commentators suggest that this increase is due to the cheaper cost of assistants than of behaviour support staff to school and (local) education authorities (Baskind and Thomson, 1995; Lee and Mawson, 1998). Whatever the reason for increased use of classroom assistants it is clear that they have potentially a valuable role to play in supporting children and young people at risk of exclusion. Poor communication between classroom assistants and mainstream teachers was identified by Lee and Mawson (1998) in their surveys, although most highlight a high degree of job satisfaction. Lee and Mawson (1998:47) conclude that the key issues for encouraging the effective uses of classroom assistants are:

* [the need for] time to be created in school for teachers and classroom assistants to meet, plan work and discuss pupils' achievements and difficulties;
* the take up of training opportunities [for classroom assistants] without any personal financial penalties;
* the recognition of the experience, expertise and qualifications of classroom assistants.

Supportive alternatives in action

In this section we move from the abstract consideration of supportive alternatives to exclusion to a consideration of three such alternatives in action in the schools involved in our exclusions research. We begin with a brief review of survey data before giving a flavour of involving parents, involving external professionals and the use of pastoral care staff. We then explore the key considerations affecting the use of alternatives to exclusion.

A wide range of support strategies to prevent pupils being excluded was reported in the survey of Scottish headteachers and reiterated in the more detailed case studies of schools. As will be seen from Table 5.1 none of these strategies is particularly innovative or experimental. They reflect well established practice in helping troubled children and the variety of contexts and kinds of trouble which are being encountered. There is thus no magic formula for preventing exclusion. Rather there is a range of approaches that can be tried in various combinations.

There are several points to make about Table 5.1. Firstly, a wide range and number of responses were given by the headteachers. At least twenty different strategies were given ranging from those with a punitive element, such as detention, to the more supportive 'help from external professionals'. Secondly, almost half the headteachers (87/167) gave more than four strategies for retaining pupils on the verge of exclusion, while others highlighted particular actions. Much depends on the pupil concerned, the resources available to the school and the values or ethos of the school. As indicated in Chapter 4, the belief in the school's function to educate all pupils went alongside a sustained effort to keep pupils in school. This commitment was as important as specific strategies. Thirdly, the strategies might be classified as 'school only', being largely under the school's control such as monitoring by senior management, and school plus, involving those outside school, most notably parents, educational professionals, and counsellors in working with the school to try to prevent exclusion. Fourthly, the label given to a particular strategy could disguise the rather different meanings ascribed to it. Involving parents, for example, can mean rather different things, from telling them to keep their child in order to working with them to develop a plan to help retain the child in school.

We give the flavour of a small number of these strategies in action before highlighting three key issues affecting the selection and use of strategies to prevent exclusion.

Involving parents

Working closely with parents to improve a young person's behaviour is often cited as an important strategy and it is no surprise to find this approach to avoiding exclusion at the top of the headteachers' list. It is also no surprise that schools involve parents in different ways

Table 5.1.   Strategies to retain pupils on the verge of exclusion

	*N	%
• involve and work with the parents	98	59
• (secondary school only) the guidance team support/monitor the pupils at risk	51	50†
• use the help of external professionals	70	42
• put the pupil on a conduct card/behaviour check/report	62	37
• use behaviour support staff or any other educational staff	54	32
• senior management checks/monitors the situation	54	32
• general discipline structure in the school	43	26
• a time out/cooling off arrangement	41	24
• the pupil's timetable and/or curriculum is modified	38	23
• individual counselling, therapeutic work with the pupils	35	21
• detention	20	12
• use of an in-school unit/base/centre	14	8
• effort/work by all the staff	15	9
• staff development	12	7
• use of alternative provision out of school, e.g. day unit	9	5
• playground strategies to avoid problems (for all pupils)	8	5
• send the pupil home if a problem occurs	7	4
• general use of extra-curricular activities, e.g. sports	5	3
• attention to the curriculum in general	3	2
• some use of home tuition	2	1

* 167 headteachers responded; this included those who were unable to give a numeric estimate of pupils at risk of exclusion. The range and complexity of the replies made it too difficult to separate out primary school from secondary school.

† Percentage of secondary headteachers.

depending on circumstances and on beliefs about what is likely to be most effective. Contacting parents once a pupil's behaviour had become a problem, but before exclusion was appropriate, was one form of involvement. Thus, for example, parents might be informed by letter or through a meeting that their child's behaviour was being monitored, or that their child had had a detention or had been allocated time in the behaviour support base. Often parents were asked to sign behaviour monitoring sheets. In some schools, parents were involved in multi-professional meetings to discuss the way forward for their child. In others, they were invited to regular meetings with appropriate school staff. Russell (1997) and Layzell (1995) describe the painstaking work in partnership with parents to establish behaviour targets for children and a common approach between home and school which had positive results. Key features were building up trust between teacher and parent, joint decision making on realistic short-term behaviour targets and recognition and reinforcement of the desired behaviour through praise. The intention behind all these ways of working seemed to be to enlist parental co-operation in supporting the school, to encourage the child to behave and to engage the child's interest in school learning.

Other ways of working with parents appeared to focus as much on parental education as on children's behaviour. Some schools had parental self-help groups run by the educational psychologist and family education schemes for parents of pupils with low self-esteem. The aim here is to improve pupil behaviour through alerting parents to particular skills and strategies and to sustain parents with children in trouble by encouraging them to share their experiences and to learn from others.

Some schools are able to provide a home visiting service which permits families to build positive relationships with schools and which can sensitise schools to family circumstances surrounding troubled behaviour. Sharp (1997) describes how a home visiting service helped to alert the secondary school to the need to review and develop its liaison with neighbouring primary schools, review its anti-bullying policy and extend its induction programme for new pupils.

A key characteristic underpinning supportive ways of involving parents is the two-way nature of the link between school and home. Parents were not only called to meetings at school, they were visited at home. Parents received letters, monitoring sheets and behaviour cards and were invited to send their comments back. Parents were involved in decisions about strategies to improve behaviour and in monitoring progress at home and in discussions comparing their child's behaviour at home and in school. The emphasis was on joint working to help a shared problem rather than apportioning blame for poor behaviour or placing untenable responsibilities on either home or school.

Involving external professionals

The use of external professionals such as educational psychologists, social workers and health visitors did not seem to relate to exclusion rates. Both high and low excluding schools and schools with no exclusions cited the help of other professionals in maintaining pupils in school at risk of exclusion. There was, however, wide variation in the way these professionals were used, including support or treatment for individual pupils, working with a group of pupils with or without a mainstream teacher, supporting groups of parents of youngsters in trouble and providing in-service training for a whole staff on class-room and playground management.

The literature identifies several problems inherent in inter-agency working. These include different views held by professionals about the origins of effective responses to troublesome behaviour, a lack of a holistic corporate framework in local (education) authorities for addressing the needs of young people and differing legislative frame-works, statutory responsibilities and budgets (Armstrong and Galloway, 1994; McKay, 1994; Kendrick, 1995; Lloyd, 1997). These mat-ters are discussed in greater detail in Chapter 6. The point to note is that involving external professionals as a strategy for preventing exclusion is not a panacea. There are different levels in which they can be involved, whole school, whole class, individual pupil, outside school working with parents, and different purposes of involvement.

As in earlier sections concerning joint working between the main-stream class teacher and the learning or behaviour support teacher or classroom assistant, time is needed for senior school staff and exter-nal professionals to work out what the purpose of joint working is and how these purposes might be achieved. For example, if the pur-pose is to raise the awareness of specific classroom management strategies, then a team-teaching approach might be appropriate. Alternatively if the main purpose is to help a specific pupil in diffi-culty then the most appropriate approach could be withdrawal of the pupil and the provision of individual support or intervention. Table 5.2 provides a summary.

External professionals might be involved in any or all of these levels. Clearly a sustained programme of involvement which has been jointly planned and developed with school staff signals a rather dif-ferent approach to supporting troubled children than single visits focusing on an individual child. In the latter case the external pro-fessional is seen as helping to provide a cure for a pupil; in the for-mer the individual help is part of a wider programme reviewing the ways in which schools can support troubled children.

Guidance staff/pastoral care

One of the most commonly cited strategies to prevent exclusion was the use of the guidance or pastoral care team in the school to moni-tor pupils at risk and to offer them support. This was a strategy avail-able only to secondary schools in Scotland since there are no specific pastoral care teams in primary schools. Pastoral care provision is organised in different ways in British schools but falls broadly into

Table 5.2.   Examples of ways of working with external professionals

Level	Contribution	Purpose
pupil	individual intervention/ support	to alleviate problems/ develop coping strategies/ form relationships
pupil group	group work intervention/ support	as above but in addition share experience, enhance social skills, self-concept and self-esteem
whole class	team teaching	develop shared perspective with teachers; introduce particular classroom management strategies
pastoral team	in-service support	to help develop counselling skills to support pupils
whole school	in-service, presentation; group work with staff; work shadowing	raise awareness of a range of practical interventions and their theoretical under-pinnings; shared perspectives
parent groups	advice/support	enhance parenting skills; share experience; enhance self-esteem; coping strategies

either a horizontal system with staff responsible for a particular year group or a vertical system where staff are responsible for a group of pupils of all ages and stages. General welfare in either system is typically the responsibility of a form tutor or 'register teacher' who sees pupils at least once a day to take the attendance register, deals with general administrative matters and takes an interest in pupils' well being. Beyond this there are promoted staff with specific responsibilities for pupils' personal, academic and vocational welfare and a senior member of staff is typically allocated strategic management responsibility for this aspect of school life.

It should be noted that there are no mandatory advanced qualifications for promoted pastoral care staff although some hold counselling or other diplomas. The time available for pastoral care staff to devote specifically to their duties varies too (most staff have subject teaching and/or management responsibilities). In addition there is discretion as to the balance of work across personal, academic and vocational matters and as between pupils in trouble and the generality of pupils. Thus decisions made in school as to the number and deployment of promoted posts allocated to pastoral care have clear implications for the amount of time and help available from this source to pupils in trouble. Furthermore, as Chapter 4 illustrated, the relationship between the operation of the guidance system and the discipline system was associated with the decision to exclude. Where the two worked closely together exclusion rates tended to be lower. Ways in which this happened included pastoral care staff conducting pupil interviews to discover their perspective on a disciplinary incident, taking part in meetings with parents (and often acting as an advocate for the parent), regular checking of behaviour monitoring sheets or through monitoring detentions and other forms of punishment. Clearly if pastoral care staff are to adopt this role as part of a strategy to combat exclusion then time and training have to be made available. The frustrations of being allocated such responsibilities without adequate resources are illustrated below:

> I have 220 pupils in my guidance group and, once I have allowed for departmental time, I have got four periods of 55 minutes each a week to do this. That includes reports, writing references, dealing with interviews with children. Now you don't deal with 220 pupils but allowing . . . half an hour an interview . . . I can see six (children) a week, if I use all my time for that. And I have got 28 cases [of pupils in difficulty] here. Now that takes until the end of October before I've got a minute to see anybody else.
>
> (Guidance teacher, Tummel Secondary School)

As we argue below, a key issue for any school wanting to provide effective alternatives to exclusion is how such alternatives are to be resourced.

Exploring why particular strategies are deployed revealed three key considerations for schools:

1. the resources available
2. perceptions of the reasons underlying difficult behaviour
3. perceptions of the effectiveness of particular ways of working.

We hope that a description of how these considerations operated in the case study schools will help others to analyse the assumptions underpinning the strategies used in particular schools.

Resources

The resources available to schools to tackle exclusion are largely dependent on central and local government policy priorities. It is clear that combating exclusion from school is part of the Labour government's programme to tackle social exclusion more generally and substantial sums have been made available to schools to take forward alternatives to exclusion projects. Such projects range from the setting up of in-school support units and bases for troubled children to ambitious plans to develop new community schools, following the 'full-services school' model in the USA. These schools are intended to promote joint working of education, health, social work and police service to encourage the participation in education of young people and their families. Many of the pilot new community schools have zero exclusion targets (Scottish Office, 1999). Structural developments to tackle exclusion require fairly substantial investment such as the provision of units and bases and the promotion of inter-agency working and form part of the current government's Alternatives to Exclusion grant. Here we are concerned with the more particular question of how schools distribute the resources allocated to them.

Schools have some degree of autonomy over how to deploy their resources of staff, time, curricular materials and physical space. Decisions about these matters can be based on custom or tradition arising from taken-for-granted assumptions about values and priorities. They can also reflect more explicit decision-making about school priorities as the following example from a primary school shows. The headteacher had consulted with staff on the subject of class sizes and had decided to reduce class sizes in the early years in the hope that habits of good behaviour would be instilled in those stages which would pay dividends later.

HT   As a staff we agreed that classes in Primary 1 and 2 [i.e. ages 5–6] are smaller classes so that difficult behaviour can be managed better and we can work on that.

I   How do you manage to get smaller classes in Primary 1 and 2?

HT   We're a priority treatment school which means we get an additional staffing allocation for classes to be smaller. What used to be done was that [we] spread that out [across the school] and instead of classes of 33 we had classes of 25. . . . Now we have upper classes that are slightly bigger – primary 7 [i.e. ages 11–12] last year was 33. . . . The staff agreed that if we got it right for younger children then the

problems will be less further on in the school. So, Primary
1 classes are about 18 and 19 and they get an element of
support through auxiliaries which we have in school.
(Headteacher, Menteith Primary School)

Senior staff in other schools made different decisions. For example,
the five extra staff allocated to Tummel Secondary School, also an area
of priority treatment, were used to decrease overall class sizes rather
than specifically to work in some way on difficult behaviour through,
for example, co-operative teaching, development of differentiated curriculum materials or employing specialist behaviour support staff.

There are, of course, many competing pressures on scarce resources.
It is important to recognise, though, that decisions made about how
to deploy resources send messages about the importance attached to
particular priorities. Thus a school which emphasises high academic
attainment as its main goal would probably have smaller classes at A
level or Higher grade rather than devote staff, time and other
resources to trying to help solve behaviour problems. For example, in
Ness Secondary School, a higher excluding academic school, the headteacher argued that:

An automatic response to an outburst from a damaged child would
not be an exclusion but it would be 'call in the experts' because we
neither have the time nor do we have the skills, because we're just
teachers basically.

So all the strategies in Table 5.1 require investment if they are to operate with any chance of success. In all schools under-achievement and
disruptive behaviour are seen as a cause for concern. The interesting
difference among schools lies in the extent to which trying to remedy
these concerns is seen as within the remit of the school and a legitimate priority, to which school resources should be devoted.

Matching causes and 'cures'

A second key issue affecting the use of alternatives to exclusion is
beliefs about the reason for troubled behaviour. Clearly if difficult
behaviour is consistently understood as something that only an expert
can resolve, then the deployment of scarce resources to support mainstream provision may seem wrong. Similarly if difficult behaviour is
seen as largely the child's own fault then punishment rather than
support can seem the logical response. There is an extensive literature on the causes and cures for troublesome behaviour (see Chapter
3; Munn and Lloyd, forthcoming). Our view is that there are some

children in schools experiencing real problems. These may be related to their lives outside school, to experiences such as loss or abuse, to relationships within the family, to cultural or peer group factors in the neighbourhood, to poverty, ethnicity, gender, to difficulties in learning, self-concept and self-esteem, to their history of learned behaviour or to school factors subsumed under the general label of ethos. As Maxwell (1995) and Capara and Rutter (1995) have suggested, it may be necessary to understand how each of this wide range may contribute and how they interact. Schools have to do the best they can in providing support and in balancing the potential complexities of causes of troubled behaviour with the strategies they have on offer. Indeed the strategies adopted will tend to reflect how staff conceptualise the problem, even when they may not know the literature on or theories underlying particular approaches to disaffected behaviour. Table 5.3 shows the strategies cited by teachers in low excluding case study schools in terms of their perceptions of the underlying reason for children's difficulties.

This list of support strategies is not intended to be comprehensive. Rather it illustrates teachers' search for a strategy (or a number of strategies) which will help best in dealing with the underlying reason for the behavioural problems.

Table 5.4 illustrates the importance of parental involvement in supporting inclusion. Where parents were seen by the headteacher as willing to accept the support which the school deemed appropriate, the pupil was not excluded. In contrast, where parents were uncommunicative and unresponsive to the support offered, the pupil was excluded. These tables illustrate something of the complexity surrounding exclusion and demonstrate that exclusion is by no means the inevitable response to challenging behaviour.

Monitoring effectiveness

Any school committed to tackling exclusion will want to monitor how effective its alternatives are. Chapter 7 discusses the conceptual difficulties in defining effectiveness as far as out-of-school provision is concerned. Some of the same problems also apply to mainstream provision. Effective for whom and in doing what are questions which schools soon confront in undertaking any serious monitoring of their practice. Thinking about effectiveness issues can help clarify for teachers, parents, pupils and other interested parties what the alternatives to exclusion hope to accomplish. Such aim-related evaluation was rare among the schools involved in our research but it did take

Table 5.3. Some support strategies cited by interviewees for pupils evincing behavioural difficulties

Teachers' perceptions of underlying reasons for behavioural difficulties

domestic background	learning difficulties	individual psychological problems	broad context of socio-economic deprivation	disaffected from school (15/16 y.o.)
• being more tolerant	• differentiated curriculum	• offering strategies for coping with e.g. anger, confrontations	• headteacher joining with health professionals to propose a local initiative to the council	• talking over problems; being open to pupils' views,
• offering time out of class as a 'haven'	• smaller classes	• counselling		• part-time schooling for 16-year-olds plus input from college, work experience, community education
• contact with parents; putting parents in touch with sources of help and advice	• co-operative teaching (more time with pupils having difficulty)	• group-work	• linking with existing projects of e.g. Family Education, Family Support Centre	• linking with Social Work's youth work
• liaison with Social Work	• use of interactive computer packages	• support in class	• senior staff acting as role models of the benefits of educational success	• clubs and leisure activities based in school
	• time in or out of class with Learning Support teacher	• educational psychologist	• work experience organised	• individually tailored programmes for achieving academic and/or vocational
	• (primary school) focus on early literacy			• links with Community Education staff to offer a more flexible curriculum
				• school leavers, 16-year-olds support group

Table 5.4.   Example of similar individual cases where one pupil was excluded and the other maintained in school

The headteacher contrasted two typical cases:

Factor level	Escalated to exclusion	Enabled inclusion
family	difficult background; mother lone parent; school seen as having no value; registered letters from school not delivered because mother refuses to answer the door; mother did not turn up to meeting at school; mother refuses help from Social Work	supportive family; despite initial scepticism, mother visited off-site support centre and spent time there helping to draw up goals etc
pupil	male; attended school despite having to get up and get his own breakfast but refused to co-operate with support offered by school	female; anti-school attitude turned around through support package (see below); reintegrated into school; stayed on after 16 and sat Highers because she realised that school could help her reach her own goals
school	behaviour support auxiliary with him for most of the time but incident occurred because support centre would not accept him on a self-referred basis – excluded because of incident. Extraordinary meeting of Support Planning Group called	school, school-based support centre and off-site support unit worked together to set up a support package of 3 afternoons in off-campus unit, 2 mornings in school support centre and remainder in school with support. Off-site unit focused on dealing with aggressive behaviour and on visualising what benefits school could offer; this was reinforced in school support centre
external support	educational psychologist involved but lack of certainty about external support available because of recent local government reorganisation; boy was much younger than others in off-site support therefore reluctant to use this option; mother refused help from social worker	

Source: interviews with teachers and senior managers in one case study school.

place. Important criteria were that the difficult behaviour stopped or was significantly reduced and that pupils settled down to normal work in the classroom. Such monitoring at the level of the individual pupil took place at regular intervals and was formalised by reporting back mechanisms to pastoral care committees or joint assessment teams in the school. Where difficulties persisted and a strategy did not work this was sometimes taken as a signal to go back to the drawing board and rethink the pupil's needs. In less flexible or imaginative schools it was the signal for longer periods of exclusion. It seemed to us that the difference between the success and failure of strategies lay not so much in the specifics of what was used. Rather the difference lay in whether an attempt was made to match the support to the underlying problems of the pupil or a routine set of responses was tried more or less automatically with little thought given to the individual pupil's situation. Much also depended on the age and stage of the pupil. Difficulties in a child of five or six may be viewed rather differently from those of a 15-year-old anxious to leave school.

At the level of the school as a whole there was regular monitoring of exclusion data. Three-quarters of the secondary schools and almost half of the primary schools involved in our research collated data. Those which did not do so had few exclusions. Having collated the data on exclusions the majority of schools used them to establish trends, to evaluate and review policy and procedures and to monitor the discipline system in the school. We came across very few schools, however, who undertook a strategic review of all their alternatives to exclusion. Rather the tendency was to monitor the effectiveness of specific initiatives such as setting up a support base, neglecting other aspects of school provision which could influence the operation of the base or whatever the specific initiative. We contend that in thinking about the usefulness of in-school alternatives to exclusion and in developing their provision, schools have a great deal to gain from a regular yearly review of them. Part of such a review should involve a collation of the records of pupils making use of alternative provision, being alert for trends in terms of age, gender and ethnicity as well as cognitive attainment. Such reviews should be the responsibility of a senior member of staff and the information provided used to inform discussion and debate about the range and success of in-school alternatives in meeting pupils' needs.

Summary

This chapter has described a range of in-school alternatives to exclusion. Some of these alternatives were categorised as punitive and as alternatives in the sense that they substituted for exclusion. These were:

- informal exclusion
- internal exclusion
- part-time school attendance.

This means that a performance management system which highlights only a reduction in exclusion numbers, risks ignoring the quality of education being offered to pupils. Familiar structural alternatives such as the use of units and bases and the use of behaviour support staff and classroom assistants were also highlighted.

A large number of in-school supportive alternatives to exclusion were reported by headteachers. Those most frequently cited tended to involve the school working with others such as parents and educational or other professionals such as psychologists, health workers and social workers. Examples were given of the different kinds of ways of working emphasising the importance of individual pupil and school circumstances in finding the most appropriate way forward. No single strategy was associated with low exclusion. Rather low excluding schools tended to use a range of approaches within an overall philosophy which valued inclusion.

Key issues in developing supportive in-school alternatives were identified as decision making about resources, beliefs about the causes of troublesome behaviour and procedures to promote a strategic review of the effectivess of in-school alternatives as well as reviewing individual cases.

We are conscious that whole-class strategies to prevent exclusion are conspicuous by their absence in this chapter, and indeed few schools in our research identified staff development in behaviour management or in using inclusive approaches as a priority. There are many practical guides and handbooks for the individual teacher wishing to reflect on his or her approach to classroom discipline and many of the whole-school approaches discussed in this chapter and in Chapter 4 have direct repercussions in the classroom. Praise and reward systems, the use of behaviour support staff and work with parents fall into this category. The provision, take-up and effectiveness of staff development opportunities in the area of behaviour management raise larger questions about the continuing professional development of teachers to which we return in the concluding chapter.

6

Supporting Pupils (and Teachers) in School to Avoid Exclusion

> I think if you can be flexible and tailor something to the individual needs of the youngsters . . . I think that's the most important thing, if you can tailor make things to suit the situation and try to put in the support that you feel would most benefit the youngster. I think that's where we get most successes.
>
> (Headteacher, Lubnaig Secondary School)

In this chapter we consider approaches to supporting pupils in mainstream school. These methods focus in general on the individual pupil. However, as argued earlier, such responses will be most effective when integrated into an overall ethos of inclusion and whole-school and classroom approaches designed to support and maintain pupils in mainstream schools. It is possible to recognise that exclusion is a social process which involves individual pupils without falling into the conceptual trap of simply individualising the problem. Exclusion is a process in which school factors play a major role; these factors include the range of methods of support for pupils, both for those who are perceived to create difficulties and those who are seen to experience difficulty.

There is a multiplicity of interacting factors, social, psychological, educational or biological, and of different theoretical accounts involved in making sense of children's actions. There are some children in schools experiencing real difficulties, sometimes related to their lives outside school, sometimes to experiences of loss, abuse or racism, to relationships within the family, perhaps to cultural or peer group factors in their neighbourhood, to poverty, ethnicity, to difficulties in learning, self-concept and self-esteem, to a history of learned behaviour in school or to school factors of ethos, curriculum, pastoral care or disciplinary structures. To understand and respond supportively to one child may involve a consideration of all of these and their dynamic interaction. Children experiencing difficulties in school may or may not be subject to formal disciplinary exclusion. Some may be excluded in other ways, either by exclusion from participation in the full range of school activities, by referral to alternative provision or by self-exclusion through non-attendance.

In previous chapters we have looked at strategies used by schools to avoid or prevent exclusion. In this chapter we concentrate on methods to support and work with individuals and groups of children both *in* difficulty and *causing* difficulty, recognising that such distinctions are difficult to sustain and that many excluded pupils have experienced difficulties in their lives which mean that a broader view of the range of pastoral and support services in school is relevant (Parsons *et al.*, 1994; Hayden, 1997). We discuss different methods of supporting individual children, the relationship of this work to that carried out by other professionals and issues about using the terms therapy and therapeutic to describe such work. We argue that there are unresolved issues of support, supervision and training for staff in schools who are working with children with both complex individual difficulties and challenging behaviour and that we need more research into the effectiveness of this work. Finally we suggest that the work of individual teachers really can make a difference to the lives of children and young people in difficulty.

Teachers are not therapists

Teachers, even pastoral care or behaviour support teachers, are not considered to be therapists. The term is usually restricted to those with a recognised professional qualification. However, it was clear from our research that many teachers are working to help and support children in school who have real and very challenging personal difficulties. Such children can be offered an experience which is therapeutic in the sense that it allows them to address and resolve issues in their lives or to feel better (Cowie and Sharp, 1998). Sometimes the relationship with an empathetic adult or peer is itself therapeutic, sometimes the adult offers more structured individual or group activities. The latter may be offered in school by pastoral care teachers, sometimes with other professionals or sometimes by outside agencies. It is important for teachers to assess their own competence in, for example, group work or counselling skills and to recognise the limits of their own skills and how they relate to those used by professionals from other agencies.

Egan (1994) describes a four stage hierarchy of helping skills (Table

Table 6.1. Hierarchy of interpersonal helping skills

Level	Training	Example
1	formal training	psychiatrists, social workers
2	trained in other professions but often called upon to help	teachers, doctors
3	public occupations but often asked to help	hairdressers, bar staff
4	effective but untrained, often called on first	family, friends, peers

6.1) with at the first level professionals who are formally trained to help, such as counsellors, psychiatrists, social workers; a second level where professionals, such as teachers, have other duties but may often be called upon to exercise helping skills; a third level where competent helping may also be offered in occupations that involve meeting the public such as bar staff, hairdressers; and the final level where effective helping may be offered by anyone such as friends or family. Often children and young people may find support or help from their peers, their family or other members of staff in the school such as playground supervisor or janitor. Helping skills can be effectively encouraged at all levels. Indeed it is sometimes argued that children prefer to be supported by 'people who acted as people and not professionals' (Lang, 1999:29). However, as we argue above, it is important for the pastoral care or behaviour support teacher to know where they fit into this range of potential support and into the continuum of help provided outwith the school.

One useful way of encouraging this kind of reflection is in the notion of a therapeutic continuum such as that below:

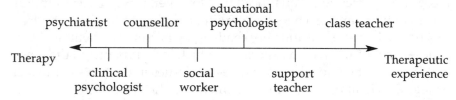

This does not mean that the children with the most difficulties are necessarily offered support at the most specialised end of the continuum. Indeed as we will argue later, sometimes teachers will be trying to help children, with for example quite severe mental health problems, in school. Often this may be because of difficulties of accessing other professional services or because of parental non-co-operation with other agencies, such as hospital psychiatric departments.

Schools can help

Schools and teachers can make a difference to children and young people, in terms of their emotional and social development and relationships, as well as their cognitive development. They can improve pupils' self-esteem, can give confidence and prevent learning problems becoming behaviour problems. For many children with difficulties in the family or community, school can be a safe and supportive refuge. Relationships with teachers can model warm and appropriate adult concern and support. The importance of educational achievement to children who are being looked after out of their original families has been often stated, although equally the educational failure of such pupils is documented (Jackson, 1987; Fletcher Campbell and Hall, 1991; HMSO, 1991; SSI/Ofsted, 1995). So success in the normal curriculum is important in supporting children with difficulties in their lives. Many pupils with individual problems can also find personal support through the ordinary range of school and class activities, such as Circle Time in the primary school (Curry and Bromfield, 1994).

> On a Monday the children were desperate to talk about what they had done at the weekend, which they did, but all sorts of things would come out about traumatic things that had happened to them as well as nice things . . . All sorts of things would come up. Issues of being honest, issues of what was upsetting the children and they just became incredibly open and there are some little devils in that class who became incredibly honest . . . It really turned the class around, it really did.
>
> (Primary 1 teacher, Katrin School, discussing use of Circle Time)

Children may find opportunities to explore difficult aspects of their lives through drama, art, free or structured play and through programmes of personal and social development.

Young Minds (1999) argue that some children who are excluded from school are likely to have unmet mental health needs. They see these as arising from a range of risk factors including poor parenting, conflict between parents, relationship breakdown, bereavement and poverty. Personal and social development programmes and attention to promoting positive social relationships/friendships in schools can be important in preventing the development of mental health problems in children and young people. Attention to the quality of work in this universal aspect of school experience can also be important in avoiding the need for more expensive individual intervention (Warden and Christie, 1997). Wilson (1996) argues that children with 'good enough' mental health will be able to deal with difficulties and learn from them. Equally a small amount of additional individual support such as that offered through Bubble Time may make a significant difference (Moseley, 1999). Many primary school class teachers may find themselves offering temporary intensive support to a child experiencing stress through, for example, loss or bereavement. Such support may be important in preventing later mental health problems (Mallon, 1998).

Counselling skills/approaches in school

> I like Mr M [support centre teacher]. If you are in trouble, instead of shouting and moaning, he talks to you and asks you what you did it for but the other teachers just start bawling and shouting.
>
> (Michael, age 13, Lubnaig School)

One professional distinction which may be important to acknowledge in a school context is that between counselling and counselling skills or counselling approaches. This is not straightforward as much of the professional literature is unclear both about the distinction between counselling and psychotherapy and between counselling, counselling skills and helping skills. Bond (1993) argues that there is currently a need for a systematic study of the differences. Sometimes counselling with children and adolescents may be seen as only involving talking, sometimes it may involve other activities such as play, drawing, or role play (Geldard and Geldard, 1997, 1999).

Much literature is reasonably clear though about a definition of what is included in formal counselling, although Bond (1993:20) argues that 'there is a closer relationship between the roles of advice, befriending, counselling skills and counselling than I had previously appreciated'. Counselling involves a formal contracting between the parties, it requires the counsellor to be trained, accredited, supervised and to operate in accordance with formal legal, ethical and professional requirements. Bond points out that the skills implied by the term 'counselling skills' are also those understood to be involved in other helping activities, social skills, interpersonal skills etc. So the terms 'counselling skills' or 'counselling approaches' imply the use of these generic skills in a process which has the same historical origins as counselling and shares some characteristics, for example, a commitment to encouraging the autonomy of the individual by allowing them to have more control of the agenda than in some of the other applications. Teachers may be using counselling skills as well as other interpersonal skills in their work.

Few teachers act, and are trained as, formal counsellors. Sometimes, but not often, formal counselling is offered by other trained professionals but more often teachers with little or no training are offering counselling skills. They may also be involved with focused, intensive individual and group work, sometimes in conjunction with a range of non-counsellor professionals, for example, social or youth workers. They are rarely professionally supervised and face some difficulty in conforming to the ethical and professional guidelines of the professional counselling bodies in some key aspects (BAC, 1999). One area where this is perhaps most problematic is that of confidentiality (Bond, 1993; Geldard and Geldard, 1999; McLaughlin, 1999). This is particularly the case with respect to the issue of child abuse, where most educational and social work establishments have clear guidelines requiring workers to refer on any disclosures of abuse by children. We will argue later in this chapter that it would be helpful for schools to develop their own supervision structures and broad ethical guidelines.

Lang quotes a teacher's comments in a recent paper on counselling, counselling skills and encouraging pupils to talk. 'You send a naughty kid to her and all she does is talk to them' (Lang, 1999:23). It may be equally thought by other staff that there is little difference between counselling and a good talking to! The headteacher below, for example, lists counselling between verbal warnings and isolation in a list of sanctions.

> Each teacher has their own way of coping with the children in the classroom and it's only when they feel that they've tried everything themselves and they're not getting anywhere then they'll go to a senior teacher for the first card but we'll recommend things like verbal warnings, counselling, isolated child, excluded groups, school teams, lines, losing points, punishment exercises, time out, letters to parents asking them to come to the teacher – these are all done in the classroom, at class level before the actual card system comes in.
>
> (Headteacher, Sween Primary School)

Teachers have an unequal power relationship with their pupils. Often teachers play a disciplinary role and may be subject teachers as well as having a pastoral care responsibility. However, much research has shown the importance to pupils of being heard by teachers in school (Sharp and Cowie, 1998; Lang, 1999; McLaughlin, 1999). If many teachers are not trained counsellors in the formal professional sense, they often offer counselling skills. This means that they pay attention to and reflect on their interpersonal relationships and in particular their listening and reflecting skills. Unconditional positive regard and empathy can be a feature of effective classroom teaching as well as counselling skills. Such skills can be developed for use by teachers but this requires training and supervision (Cowie and Pecherek, 1994).

Most courses on counselling skills undertaken by teachers are likely to be based on a broad and fairly eclectic theoretical model such as that of Egan (1994). However, sometimes such training may be offered in a person-centred or psychodynamic theoretical framework. It is important for teachers who are working with children and young people in difficulty to recognise that there are theoretical differences which are reflected in differences in practice. This may be crucial in understanding why a psychologist or other professional is recommending a particular course of action. Understanding different theoretical models may also be helpful for pastoral care staff in selecting a strategy for their own use. As we argued earlier, individual teachers will tend to choose to respond according to their own explanation of the pupil's behaviour. Equally class or subject teachers may be more or less sympathetic to a pupil's circumstances according to how they are communicated. A member of staff in a social work and education support unit working with a secondary school in our research, talked of the importance of school staff having access to the minutes of the meetings of the school joint assessment team, so that they would know which children were discussed and have some idea of both the reasons underlying the behaviour and the proposed responses:

> where the staff feel that there is something being done, where they feel there's a plan, where they feel people are trying to solve a problem they'll go through fire and water for the pupil. Where they have no idea why this is occurring in the class they just see it as a personal attack on them, then they're much less sympathetic . . .
> (Co-ordinator social work/education project, Tummel High School)

Table 6.2 shows examples of activities which might be associated with particular theoretical models. There are problems, however, in reducing complex theoretical perspectives into a table form. They are inevitably simplified. Sometimes particular methods can be seen to fit clearly into one of the major psychological perspectives; others do not clearly belong to one particular theoretical perspective or may contain elements drawn from different models.

Some methods, for example counselling, group work, family work, can be offered in a psychodynamic, cognitive, or person-centred

Table 6.2.   Theories and methods

	The main psychological models
Psychodynamic	Stress on understanding, on behaviour having a history and on recognition of the inner world of both child and teacher. Emphasis on feelings and processes. Methods include counselling skills, group work and psychodrama.
Person-centred	Emphasises person's striving to feel positive about themselves. Role of the worker is to facilitate this. Optimistic in belief that characteristic of human being to wish to feel better about their life. Focus on self-esteem. Methods include counselling skills, group work.
Humanistic	Related to person-centred approach, in emphasis on self-concept and promoting self-esteem. Idea of universal basic needs, often expressed as a hierarchy from physical needs to social and psychological. Methods include nurture groups, activities to promote self-esteem.
Behavioural	Inappropriate behaviour is learned and can be measured and modified. Concentrates on observable behaviour rather than inner world. Methods include teaching/ rewarding appropriate behaviour. Social skills training.
Cognitive behavioural	This approach also sees behaviour as learned but emphasises the relationship between beliefs/attitudes and behaviour. Sets out to enable pupils to see and learn to control the relationship between their thoughts and behaviour. Methods include teaching pupils specific strategies for self/impulse control and for monitoring their own behaviour.
	Approaches drawing on various models
Approaches associated with emotional intelligence/literacy	Methods include strategies for developing empathy, impulse control, pro-social actions
Brief therapy/solution focused approaches	Mainly cognitive based but may draw on other models. 'What's the trouble? If it works do more of it. If it doesn't work, stop doing it. Do something different.' (Quick, 1996:2) Methods include problem free talk, formulating strategies based on child's visualisation of a 'better' life and on 'exceptions' when things go well.
Eco-systemic approaches	Based on view of pupil as centre of a system, involving different people, with different perspectives on the problem. Methods include observation, interviewing participants in the system, 'sleuthing' where teachers and pupils explore perceptions.
Social education approaches	These often draw on humanistic or person-centred approaches, with more emphasis on understanding behaviour in its social and cultural context and working with children's difficulties within that context, for example in the peer group or through activities which pupils would choose. Methods include group work, peer group supports, befriending and often using games and exercises in a climate of enjoyment as well as social learning. Emphasis on support without labelling.

framework. The method of intervention or support chosen, as argued above, will reflects the worker's understanding of the origins of or background to the child's difficulties. Most teachers and social workers are eclectic – they pick the approach which makes sense to their understanding and fits best with their own style. A teacher may find the psychodynamic perspective helpful in *understanding* why a boy with a history of rejection by his mother is constantly angry with his female teacher but use a cognitive behavioural approach in *helping* the boy develop strategies to deal with his behaviour. She may, of course, first have explored whether the boy is angry because of his experiences with the teacher in the classroom. Listening to the boy make sense of his own situation would be the starting point for most approaches.

Many methods used in schools also incorporate sociological insights, e.g. about the importance of peer groups in influencing behaviour, or viewing the actions of an individual as part of a system of inter-related structures, including family, community and school. Equally some approaches might stress understanding the local culture of the school's neighbourhood. Sometimes behaviour is seen as having a biological origin, modifiable through the use of drug therapy. Often this method will be associated with other strategies, for example based on cognitive behavioural models.

Understanding the background to difficult behaviour can make teachers more sympathetic to individual pupils. Equally listening to children by using counselling skills can also help teachers gain a clearer understanding of the feelings of children involved, for example, in exclusion, as well as offering support to the child. There are, as we have argued, clear issues about training and supervision of teachers using counselling and other helping skills. However, it is clear that the proper use of these skills in schools can be highly effective in contributing to a successful, inclusive approach to children and young people in difficulty.

Preventing exclusion by teaching pupils specific survival skills

Some schools have developed programmes focused on interpersonal violence, as a way of preventing the need to resort to exclusion. Much work on this in schools depends on the idea that pupils can be helped to develop strategies to manage their own behaviour in school and learn to avoid disruptiveness in class or becoming involved in violence. Often this is based on a behavioural, or cognitive-behavioural, theoretical model, which sees the child's behaviour as a learned response and aims to enable the learning of a more appropriate response to certain situations. Sometimes pupils are encouraged to write their own behavioural objectives and to identify an appropriate reward for success. This may take the form of a behavioural contract. The essence of success in such contracts is that the pupil perceives some benefit as well as the school, that all parties have a say in its composition and that they should be renegotiable (Ayers *et al.*, 1995). Behavioural monitoring charts, sheets or books also seem to be more effective if pupils have contributed to their compilation. Often these are shared on a regular basis with parents.

> He attends a support centre and has a conduct/behaviour sheet which keeps me in contact with what he is doing in class and how his behaviour is which is a good idea. I like that because I can see what he's doing and what he's not doing and they tell me how he's behaved that day.
>
> (Mrs N., mother of Michael, Lubnaig Secondary School)

Behaviour self-management methods also emphasise the importance of the involvement of the pupil. Some earlier behavioural approaches, still sometimes used in schools, involve teacher assessment of behaviour and teacher design and implementation of a behavioural programme (Merrett and Merrett, 1992; Traxson, 1994; Anderson and Merrett, 1997). Anger management courses often involve the teaching of a combination of self-management and problem-solving skills, assertiveness and relaxation techniques. Michael, also quoted earlier, from Lubnaig School, was clear about why he was angry.

> My mum used to get battered all the time and my sister got sexually abused by my step dad. Ever since that, I've always been angry about things. . . I used to go to [anger therapist]. It's like this woman, she thingummies your anger. She's meant to take it away. It's meant to relax you. I used to go to that but I stopped going because I was missing too much school because after it I was tired and greeting [crying] and things like that. . . When I get angry, I've got a really bad temper but I've sort of calmed down and try not to. It helped a little.

Many of the available packages have been developed for use with young male offenders and successful programmes seem to have been part of a multi-modal approach to intervention (Farrington, 1995; McGuire, 1997), that is as part of a range of other strategies including perhaps work with parents, group work or work placement. Often this work takes place in schools within support groups of selected young people who take part in role play of potentially difficult situations and model less angry responses. In one case study school in our exclusions research, a principal teacher of guidance in Fyne Secondary School described an anger management group which he felt had been helpful, but expressed concern over the amount of his time involved:

> what I did with B H, the psychologist, last year, was we had one group that was basically anger control, and we had a group of 5 girls from my year, who had severe difficulties with just losing it in classes and tried to teach them techniques. Now that was not entirely successful, we still have one or two who flip occasionally but it made a big difference but it was intensive, it took at least an hour of my time every week for those 5 pupils for 7 or 8 weeks and then we went back and did a recall so that is expensive on your time.

One issue identified by a school social worker, working in another school-based anger management group, was that during the life of the group several of its members were excluded. This account also points to some of the difficulties of inter-professional communication discussed earlier in this book.

> I don't know about the exclusion until after the event so I turn up for the group on a Thursday morning and find that three out of the five kids have been excluded.
>   (School social worker, Lubnaig Secondary School)

This is a graphic reminder of the importance of decision-making structures and procedures about exclusion raised in Chapter 3. It also points to the contradictions often apparent in schools like Lubnaig, where this can happen despite a real attempt by some staff to be inclusive (Clark *et al.*, 1999).

O'Rourke and Worzbyt (1996) recommend strategies for developing empathy, impulse control, problem-solving skills, behavioural skills and specific anger management strategies. They define empathy as the ability to identify with the emotional state of others, to see through the eyes of another and to respond to the emotional state of another. In the USA, approaches to this are often associated with the idea of emotional intelligence or emotional literacy (Goleman, 1996; Sharp and Cowie, 1998).

Conflict resolution schemes can involve peer mediation or can be managed by school staff. They are based on the argument that peer group problems can be most effectively resolved by non-punitive strategies (Stacey, 1996; Sharp and Cowie, 1998). Sharp and Cowie (1998) provide a detailed account of mediation approaches and identify three key concepts which underpin this kind of work. These are first that conflict is not bad and can be constructive; second that conflict is not a contest and that it can be resolved using 'win-win' solutions; and third that it is necessary to distinguish between what people want and why they want it, enabling focus on the needs underpinning behaviour. Strategies for dealing with conflict are also often developed through peer support group work (O'Rourke and Worzbyt, 1996).

Group work

Much of the successful support for, or intervention with, individual pupils that was described in our research involved group work. This has been very widely developed and used in Scotland, sometimes taking place in school or offered outside school by youth or social work projects (Lloyd, 1992). In one authority it was still called intermediate treatment, a term used widely in Britain in the 1970s and 1980s but now less widely employed.

> Shona likes the IT [intermediate treatment]. She's quite good at attending that regularly and she's got genuine support there . . . As I say, I find that at IT they are always genuine. They are really quite helpful and they always let me know how she is progressing and what have you.
>
> (Mrs E., mother of Shona, attending intermediate treatment evening group)

Group work is based on the recognition that children and young people have something to offer each other. It can create an atmosphere that is conducive to getting in touch with relevant feelings and issues and sharing them with a group of peers. It enables children and adolescents to contribute more, work with and for each other. 'Jointly working on one person's problems has the effect of influencing everyone else's in the group' (Dwivedi, 1993:10). Groups may be intended to foster general confidence or self-esteem, may be focused on specific issues such as bereavement or family problems or they may involve developing general or particular social skills such as anger management. Group work may involve mainly discussion but more often methods include structured activities, games, drama and role play (Bond, 1986; Brandes, 1982; Quayle and Holdsworth, 1997).

Humour and a relaxed, more facilitative intervention style by adults are often perceived to be both one strength of group work but also an aspect which may be more problematic for teachers who are also responsible for more formal aspects of school life. Several teachers in our research also found that colleagues sometimes perceived such activities as rewarding the 'bad' behaviour of pupils.

> That group would do a mixture of being in the building doing social skills like games and exercises and going out on activities and there's a feeling in the school that that's a sort of group where it's treats for kids who are not behaving.
>
> (Guidance teacher, Lubnaig Secondary School)

This highlights a critical difficulty for staff trying to maintain children in school and avoiding exclusion.

> In some respects, it's also hard to get some of the guidance teachers identifying with what's happening and who should be part of the group but I think, in fact I know, that there is some resistance to referring because people feel kids don't deserve it, you know, that basically they shouldn't be in the school anyway, they should be elsewhere.
>
> (School social worker, Lubnaig Secondary School)

Some schools have attempted to avoid such issues and also the potentially stigmatising effect of group membership by offering group experiences more openly to other pupils. One of the schools in our research ran a group work scheme called the 'adventure service team' which consisted of 60 per cent referred young people and 40 per cent who were:

> your average kid in the school who is interested in what we are offering . . . it's a new kind of intervention from our point of view in that it's run along similar lines as a youth club. You use a brief therapy model of running the group, where we basically try to pick up on strengths that kids have with the intention, that if they improve their confidence and skills in lots of areas then ... this will reduce their need to gain kudos in negative ways within the school.
>
> (Teacher in school based support unit, Tummel School; see below for discussion of brief therapy)

During our research the issue of gender was raised in relation to group work. There was concern to avoid groups with, as one teacher put it: 'eight disruptive boys and two girls'. As argued later, in Chapter 7, much special provision for children in difficulty, in or out of mainstream school, is dominated by large numbers of boys. Some of those offering group work had taken account of gender differences when planning activities. For example they sometimes ran single sex groups or, where they were mixed, they made sure that the activities reflected the interests of both boys and girls. In accounts of practice in the UK there is surprisingly little reference to the aspects of gender or ethnicity in work with pupils with emotional or behavioural difficulties, despite the significance of these factors in understanding why certain children are excluded and/or identified with emotional or behavioural difficulties. In our research, when heads were asked to talk about the salient features of exclusion very few mentioned gender, social class or culture.

The group work scheme described above used a 'brief therapy' approach, sometimes also described as solution-focused intervention. This method implies a criticism of much work with disruptive and/or excluded children and their families, when too much time is uselessly spent on discussing the problem rather than finding positive ways forward. Teachers and others using this approach try to generate 'problem-free talk', encouraging the visualisation of a 'better' life (de Shazer, 1991; Rhodes and Ajmal, 1995; Quick, 1996).

It is argued that this approach has been successful for a number of reasons. It is optimistic and can offer visible, short-term results but, perhaps more importantly, it encourages the other professionals involved with the child to make an effort to perceive their positive achievements. This emphasis on the positive fits with some approaches to positive discipline in schools which emphasise catching pupils being 'good'. In our research Mrs N., whose son Michael had been regularly excluded, said how she valued the feedback from the teacher in the support centre, who emphasised Michael's positive achievements:

> It lets me know everything that has been going on that Michael has not told me. It also lets me know how the rest of the teachers feel about it. Some, I think, see him bad all the time; they don't see the good side, it's always the bad side of him they see but Mr L. sees the good side and the other teachers he works with see the good side.

Table 6.3 gives a summary of some of the methods used in schools to work with or support pupils causing or experiencing difficulties in school.

Table 6.3. Some methods to support/work with pupils in difficulty or causing difficulty in school

Available in classrooms	What this might involve
Relationships with teachers.	Warm adult concern, direction.
Support through curriculum.	Circle time.
Teaching social skills.	Role play, discussion of situations.
Listening to individuals.	Counselling skills or bubble time.
Behaviour management approaches.	Targets, behaviour sheets.
Extra support in times of stress.	Understanding loss/bereavement.
Enhancing self-esteem.	Achievement, recognition.

Additional strategies	What this might involve
Counselling skills from pastoral care staff.	Listening, empathy, positive regard.
Group work.	Sharing difficulties, games, role play.
Anger management programmes.	Learning impulse control, role play.
Conflict mediation.	Learning empathy, social skills practice.
Peer counselling.	Pupils offer basic counselling skills.
Behaviour contracts.	Agreement with pupil and parents.
'Brief therapy.'	Solution-focused problem solving.
Cognitive behavioural approaches.	Target setting from self assessment.
Involvement of external agency.	Social work, educational psychologist.
Individual timetable.	Avoid problem classes.
Out-of-school placement.	Work experience, broaden experience.
Referral to outside agency.	Mental health services, youth agencies.

Dilemmas and issues for schools and teachers

Several pastoral care and behavioural support teachers in our study mentioned the pressure they felt when seeking to provide both proper, but time-consuming, support for individual children and to continue to manage the rest of their work. This may be one reason for the recent popularity of solution-focused approaches which offer the possibility of a more rapid resolution of problems. Ethical principles associated with the use of counselling skills are often quoted as beneficence, non maleficence, justice and respect for autonomy (Bond, 1993). These can all be challenged by the situation where the teacher has to balance the right of the individual pupil against the entitlement of her/his peers. The best interests of one individual can be set against the welfare of the rest. This argument is often used in schools where, for example, exclusion is used. In such circumstances, the guidance teacher may find him or herself supporting excluded pupils on their return to school where the pupils may reasonably argue that the exclusion was not in their best interests, that they were harmed by it, that it was unfair and that it did not contribute to their greater autonomy. It may be difficult, sometimes, for pastoral care teachers not to feel that their integrity has been compromised. Such staff do have to fulfil many different roles and a trade-off in terms of their potentially conflicting demands is inevitable. Children and young people may still ask for help and support from the teachers who can therefore be involved in both an excluding and a supportive role. It is important therefore for schools to recognise this issue in reviewing the relationship and balance between their pastoral care and disciplinary structures.

There was a sense in several schools in our research that they were moving in two simultaneous but conflicting directions. At the same time as there was pressure to demonstrate improvement in academic achievement, some teachers felt that they were having to provide more personal support for pupils in difficulty.

> I remember in B [former school in very disadvantaged neighbourhood], we coped with children with behaviour problems, we had to, and you had a lot of sympathy for them and you could see why they were doing this and how insecure and unconfident and their lack of self-esteem but it meant that the kids who didn't have all these problems suffered because all the attention was going towards one or two pupils.
>
> (Principal teacher, English, Ken School)

When discussing pupils with emotional or behavioural difficulties in England, Cooper (1999:30) argues that the work undertaken by teachers and others takes place in 'persistently deteriorating circumstances: as the knowledge, practice and skills of professionals increase so do the challenges with which they have to cope'. This may lead to teachers feeling a conflict between different aspects of their work. As pastoral care teachers, many may feel torn between support for their colleagues facing real difficulties in the classroom and their responsibility towards individual pupils. It is possible, however, to develop structures to support both pupils and teachers in schools. This would require a perspective that acknowledges that individual pupils may behave in ways that are difficult or disturbing to teachers and that there are real issues facing schools in supporting troubled and troublesome children but that it is still possible to offer unconditional positive regard for such pupils. There is little point in the guidance or pastoral care teacher having unconditional positive regard in using counselling skills with pupils if the pupils feel that the rest of the school has no regard for them. Equally teachers may not be able to employ these skills if they themselves feel unsupported in school. Cole *et al.* (1998) emphasise the crucial importance of the belief of heads and senior management in the rights of all pupils to be equally valued and to experience empathy from staff, even when the tolerance of the staff is challenged.

In Chapter 4 we argued that such belief is a key feature of the ethos of inclusive schools.

Many professionals, teachers and others, in schools working with some of the most difficult children, do not receive any form of support or supervision in relation to their use of counselling skills in individual work or in group work. Many teachers are working in school with children with very challenging behaviour or with significant mental health problems. Sometimes, but by no means always, such pupils may be receiving help from other professionals outside school. There was a sense in some of the schools we visited in our research that teachers felt they were the front-line with these pupils, often unable to obtain further assistance.

Teachers who are working in an identified role using group work, counselling skills and other helping skills with troubled or troublesome children could be seen to require the following:

- personal support in dealing with the stress of the work
- encouragement to engage in professional development and training
- assistance in sorting out personal, professional and organisational boundary issues
- help in identifying ethical issues and dilemmas in their work
- reflection on when they are using counselling skills
- help in identifying issues to do with culture, gender and power
- encouragement to explore the theoretical underpinning of their work
- help in identifying when some work is inappropriate/too difficult/should be referred elsewhere
- information about the law including the rights of children and parents in education and social welfare.

(Lloyd, 1999:29)

Some issues and dilemmas faced by school staff might be helpfully addressed if schools were to develop their own ethical position statements about working with children in difficulty in a school setting. The position statements could include a statement of ethics and practice, in particular in relation to confidentiality and information sharing, a statement of aims and philosophy of counselling and helping skills. Equally useful in promoting consistent and effective working would be a description of administrative practice, for example record keeping, an account of the arrangements for the delivery of work, guidelines for working with other professionals, managing the boundaries of different professional responsibility and the arrangements for supervision of pastoral care and behaviour support staff.

Conclusion: teachers can make a difference for individual children in difficulty

Sharp and Cowie (1998) finish their valuable book on counselling and supporting children in distress with the story of an old man on a beach throwing starfish back into the sea to save them from being dried up by the sun. A passing young man pointed to the thousands on the beach and asked how he could hope to make a difference. The old man looked at the starfish in his hand and said 'I make a difference to this one' (Sharp and Cowie, 1998:139). In a recent research project involving young women who had been identified as having social, emotional or behaviour problems at school one respondent, 'Ann', talked of her secondary school learning support teacher. Ann had experienced distressing abuse in her family and in care and had truanted from school for long periods. Finally in her last care placement she returned to school and was introduced to 'Sophia', a learning and behaviour support teacher who was experienced in counselling skills.

> So I turned up and at first I was sitting there going 'I cannae do it, I cannae do it', but Sophia she was fabulous she gave me a great pushing and I really did work hard in the learning support and I caught up with all my work. Considering that I missed near enough three, four years of school while I was here, there and everywhere, she really did help me quite a bit because I got better grades in my exams than some of the other kids who had been there every day. So it's Sophia I've got to thank, she was really brilliant and there were a number of times when I just couldn't take it and she always gave me another chance.
>
> (Lloyd and O'Regan, 1999:42)

Three years later Ann is working and managing her life successfully. She is quite clear that it was meeting that one supportive teacher that made the difference. She always gave her another chance.

Several writers on inclusion make the important point that the achievement of supportive settings in mainstream schools is always a formidable task, that progress will rarely be linear and is more likely to be patchy (Cole *et al.*, 1998; Clark *et al.*, 1999). Good practice with pupils with emotional and behavioural difficulties can reflect the values and ethos of the school as argued in Chapter 4. Approaches to work with individual children in difficulty are most successful when fully integrated into the work of the school. This chapter has mentioned some of the methods used to support and work with children who are difficult or in difficulty in school and identified the need for support and training for staff working with such pupils. The complex relationship is also recognised between the idea of exclusion and that of special educational needs and in particular the use of the labels Emotional and Behavioural Difficulty and Special Educational Needs. Equally we recognise that we are discussing a diverse range of pupils. Gender, class and ethnicity are relevant to understanding who is excluded from school or placed in special provision as a result of difficulties in school. These factors need then also to be built into thinking about appropriate responses to individual children. As we saw earlier, for example, methods like group work involving a majority of boys may not be appropriate for a minority of girls.

Schools can offer a great deal to support their pupils, however labelled, through a range of different strategies and while there are no magic answers, there is evidence, as Lane (1994) argues, that some things do work for some children. Effective responses to difficult behaviour cannot be rigidly prescribed. It was clear in our research that patience, imagination and flexibility were crucial in finding the best way to support an individual pupil. Successful intervention was based on the recognition that disruptive behaviour can be related to different problems in children's lives and therefore particular strategies might work because they made sense for that child in that school. This also underlines the central importance of fully including pupils and families in the discussion of how best to support them.

7

Out of School – How Effective Are Alternatives to Inclusion?

I have to admit we have in fact excluded somebody to ensure that the authority does act to find alternative provision for them, particularly when they read the background.

(Headteacher, secondary school)

Despite the current policy emphasis on inclusion in Britain there are still considerable numbers of pupils not included in mainstream school, because of their temporary or permanent disciplinary exclusion from school or because they have been placed in special provision for emotional or behavioural difficulties. All of these pupils are excluded, in any broad sense of the term, from participation in mainstream education. This chapter looks at the nature of the schooling for these pupils and at issues of effectiveness of alternative educational provision. This chapter is based on a review of recent research and literature which was conducted in association with our exclusions study (Cullen and Lloyd, 1997). It raises questions about the continued relevance of alternative provision and the standards by which it can be judged. We argue that the evidence which is available on the effectiveness and on outcomes of special provision suggests that, while there may be strongly held views on the need for this provision, its use and value should be subject to question.

The Scottish HMI (1990) concluded that it was not easy to measure the effectiveness of schooling for pupils with (social) emotional or behavioural difficulties. This has been echoed in more recent publications (Cole *et al.*, 1998; Grimshaw and Berridge, 1994). Cole and his colleagues in their recent study questioned whether it was possible to apply the notions of effectiveness developed in relation to mainstream schooling, 'whether HMI are right in seeing no essential differences between effective teaching of mainstream children in "ordinary

111

schools" and pupils with EBD in special schools' (Cole *et al.*, 1998:19). Clearly any discussion of alternative provision has also to be contextualised within wider debates both about the aims, purposes and effectiveness of mainstream schooling and about the concept of special educational needs and ideas of inclusion.

What counts as alternative provision?

The literature on the effectiveness of alternative provision for pupils excluded from school is difficult to delineate. At one and the same time, it is a narrow topic (because effectiveness is under-researched) and a vast topic (because the nature of provision varies widely – from group work with a local youth worker to residential schooling, from a special unit in the neighbourhood to secure accommodation or a psychiatric unit in hospital). It is also a topic which easily strays into other areas because exclusion from school carries social consequences: for example, excluded pupils are more likely to commit offences (Audit Commission, 1996) therefore the literature on juvenile delinquency is potentially relevant; they are also more likely to be in care before exclusion and to be taken into care as a result of exclusion, therefore the burgeoning literature on that topic also becomes relevant.

It does not make sense to consider only such provision as is made for pupils officially excluded from school because of their perceived indiscipline, for example Pupil Referral Units (which in any case do not exist in Scotland), as many children who are placed in other forms of special provision have experienced exclusion. Some commentators argue that any child or young person not in mainstream school for any reason is effectively excluded, regardless of whether a legal disciplinary sanction has been applied (Booth, 1996). Here we take a middle course, considering alternative provision made for pupils who are outwith mainstream either because of behaviour considered unacceptable in mainstream and/or perceived problems relating to 'social, emotional or behavioural difficulties' in Scotland and 'emotional and behavioural difficulties' in England. This focus is wider than on alternative provision following official exclusion as a legal sanction but not so wide as to encompass, for example, provision primarily intended for physical or sensory disabilities. It does imply rejection of the apparently easy distinction reflected in some English provision, between disruptive pupils and pupils with emotional and behavioural difficulties, between 'ordinary bad behaviour and disturbed behaviour' (DES, 1989 para 6.30). Armstrong and Galloway (1994) demonstrate the practical and theoretical difficulties created by attempting to sustain this simplistic distinction in the real processes of assessment and placement in alternative provision.

Alternative provision begins once a pupil is out of mainstream school for all or part of the time. Thus it includes provision where the pupil is in school some of the time but receives alternative education somewhere else for the rest of the week. An example might be part-time in school and part-time in an off-campus unit or youth strategy centre (Simpson, 1992). It also includes all provision where the pupil is out of mainstream full time whether or not the provision made is itself part or full time. Hence it includes home tuition and pupil refer-ral units, both of which have tended to be part time – this is now changing – as well as day and residential provision in special schools, day or residential provision in hospital settings, residential provision in secure and psychiatric units (Parsons *et al.*, 1995; DfEE, 1999).

Often this range of provision is represented by a triangle, where the broad base represents mainstream school with or without support, and which gradually tapers through day provision to residential pro-vision before closing at the apex of secure provision for a tiny min-ority of pupils. One version of such a representation is set out in Figure 7.1. Sometimes provision is represented as a continuum, from least to most segregated.

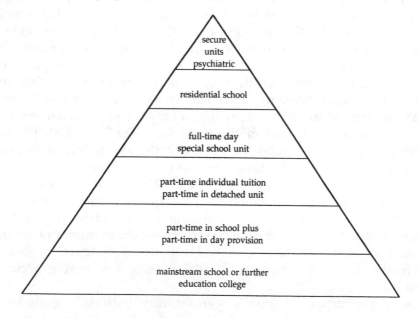

Figure 7.1. Representation of the range of provision

Such neat representations are deceptive in a number of ways. First, they fail to represent the fact that some pupils who are excluded from mainstream obtain no alternative provision. This is likely to be the case for most pupils out of mainstream on short, temporary exclusions. For some pupils, possibly the majority of all pupils excluded, this will not matter a great deal since their exclusion may last for only a few days before a full return to school is made and is likely never to be repeated (Cullen *et al.*, 1996). For these pupils, the educational loss may be comparable to that of an absence due to a short illness. For other pupils, lack of any alternative educational provision will be more serious, either because their exclusion continues for weeks or even months, or because the temporary exclusion is repeated frequently (Mitchell, 1996). For a third, very small, group of excluded pupils, mainly permanently excluded pupils (excluded, removed from the register in Scotland), the lack of any alternative provision is disastrous. They are lost from the educational system down the gaps and cracks in the provision of alternative education (Mitchell, 1996; Stirling, 1994; Ofsted, 1993).

Alternative provision is not, then, a neat extension of the mainstream base. There is potential for there to be a clear gap between mainstream and any alternative provision. This has been recognised by government and clearer guidance about the duties of education authorities has been issued in England and Wales (DfEE, 1999) and in Scotland (Scottish Office, 1998). In England and Wales, that guidance stipulates that, 'a headteacher considering excluding a pupil for a single block of more than 15 school days in a term must plan: to enable the pupil to continue their education; how to use the time to address the pupil's problems; and, with the local education authority, what educational arrangements will best help the pupil to reintegrate into the school at the end of the exclusion' (DfEE, 1999:32–33). In addition the guidance states that, by 2002, the aim is that all pupils excluded for more than 15 days in one term will receive full-time and appropriate education whilst excluded. The guidance from the Scottish Office (1998:7–9) reminded authorities of 'their continuing obligations in respect of children who have been excluded ... authorities need to have available a range of provision to meet a range of needs. That range should be specified and may include school based or off-site provision for pupils at risk of being – or having been – excluded.'

For a proportion of pupils permanently excluded (excluded, removed from the register in Scotland) from one mainstream school, alternative provision is made for them in another mainstream school.

Parsons *et al.* (1995:21) found this was the case for 27 per cent of primary and 15 per cent of secondary pupils excluded permanently. Indeed, they suggested that this was an underestimate of possibly as much as a further 25 per cent. This underestimation resulted from a combination of poor record keeping in some LEAs, and a policy, in other LEAs, of swiftly placing pupils in a new school without noting these cases. The fact that many pupils permanently excluded from one school settle in another school reinforces the importance of the issue of qualitative differences between mainstream schools in terms of ethos, of curriculum provision, teacher–pupil relations and parental involvement.

For the majority of temporarily excluded pupils no alternative provision is made in the sense that the outcome of exclusion is a quick return to their original school. For example, in our research on exclusion, we found that of our sample (which was drawn from 'high' and 'low' excluding schools and so is not representative) 74 per cent of secondary and 83 per cent of primary pupils excluded temporarily returned to their original school (Cullen *et al.*, 1996). Thus the range of alternative provision is relevant for only a minority of excluded pupils, who are themselves, in turn, a minority of all pupils.

Perhaps the most important rider to the neat triangular representation of alternative provision shown in Figure 7.1 is that it does not convey a sense of the varied gaps which exist in provision according to locality (see, e.g., HMI, 1990; Chisholm, 1987; Hill *et al.*, 1995). Nor does it indicate clearly that pupils do not always move slowly through an 'obstacle course' of support and provision designed to prevent them reaching the sharp end of residential or secure provision. Sometimes it is felt this approach is not appropriate and a child goes from mainstream directly into provision near or at the apex of the triangle; sometimes the range of provision does not exist in a locality and a child zooms from mainstream to residential for no other reason (MacIver and Martin, 1987). The range of alternative provision which is considered in relation to a given pupil is, then, highly dependent on the provision which exists locally. It will be interesting to monitor improvements in this situation as a result of the clearer guidance to authorities noted above.

Standards of effectiveness?

The effectiveness of anything is judged by its power to produce consequences; that these should be desired consequences is understood. Clearly it is worthwhile to assess the effectiveness of alternative provision because, as Topping (1983) argues, its existence costs a lot of taxpayers' money and has significance for the lives of all those involved, particularly the children in it. However, as argued earlier the issue of the effectiveness of alternative provision is not straightforward. In this section some of the main standards which set out the 'desired consequences' of alternative provision are introduced. Key arguments suggesting the problems involved in trying to judge the effectiveness of alternative provision then follow.

Based on the literature reviewed, it seemed that three different, though related, sets of 'desired consequences' were being used as the standards by which the effectiveness of alternative provision was assessed. These standards are:

• adherence to key principles
• fulfilment of aims and objectives
• meeting individual needs.

Under educational law, schools may exclude pupils if it is believed that their continued presence in the school compromises the educational well-being of their peers. The right of the majority to be educated in safety, within an ordered and disciplined environment, is thus one standard by which the effectiveness of alternative provision may be judged. Thus, alternative provision may be deemed effective if it can be shown that its existence allows mainstream schools to be free from disruption. The problem with using this as a standard is that the present law reflects an understanding of behaviour which is no longer regarded as adequate. The child-deficit idea of behaviour, which is reflected in the law on exclusion, sees the source of disruption as within the child involved. This view does not account for the contextual nature of behaviour. As we argued in earlier chapters the behaviour of its pupils is influenced by the structure and ethos of schools. The current exclusion law does not reflect the mass of evidence which shows that disruptive behaviour occurs within a particular context. Removing one pupil may change the context to an extent, but it will not solve the underlying strains which allow disruption to occur within a school. It could be argued that the right of the majority of pupils to an education in a safe, ordered and disciplined environment may be better safeguarded by focusing on school culture, rather than on individual pupils within that culture.

Under the UN Convention, ratified by the UK, children have a right to adequate provision, to protection from abuse, to participation in decisions affecting them, and to express their views. Some writers suggest that this should be used as a standard by which to judge the effectiveness of alternative provision. For example, MacPhee (1992) suggests that the effectiveness of the process of assessment for alternative provision could be judged by its adherence to the rights of the child. To date, however, while children's rights have influenced recent social welfare legislation (The Children Act 1989, and The Children (Scotland) Act 1995), there has been no reflection of this in law relating to education (Lloyd, 1997). Thus, while this argument is important in highlighting, among other things, the discrepancies between the law in two key areas relating to the welfare of children and young people, it could be argued that, in the meantime, it is unreasonable to judge alternative educational provision by a standard which is not upheld by education law. This is further complicated, of course, by the existence of residential and day social work funded establishments with educational provision, admission to which is through social work/juvenile justice procedures, based on social welfare legislation.

Some writers argue that the effectiveness of alternative provision should be judged against principles based on clear value positions relating to the equality of human worth. Thus, organisations such as the Centre for the Study of Integration in Education (CSIE), as well as internationally agreed statements, such as the Salamanca Statement, argue that alternative provision per se is an infringement of human rights. They argue that all children have a right to education within a mainstream environment. If this position is accepted, the effectiveness of alternative provision can only be judged in negative terms – how much or how little infringement of this basic principle particular forms involve.

Another key principle which is put forward as a standard by which to judge alternative provision is the principle of least intrusion. Sometimes this is stated as the principle of the least restrictive environment. The argument here is that interventions which least disrupt and constrain the family and community networks of the child will always be the preferred option which should be acted upon if possible. This argument informed, for example, the aims of Lothian's youth strategy (LRC, 1989) and of Scottish social work policy on child protection (Kendrick, 1995). On the other hand, as Kendrick points out, it has been argued that this principle can lead to romanticised notions of supportive families and communities which bear little resemblance to day-to-day reality for some children and young people. It has also been criticised by writers arguing for the residential sector of alternative provision as being ideologically, rather than evidentially, based (Priestley, 1987). In some cases, it is argued, it has prevented major intervention being used appropriately at an early stage. Thus, taken alone, this principle may not be a sufficient standard by which to judge the effectiveness of alternative provision.

It seems reasonable to argue that the effectiveness of any educational provision should be judged by the aims and purposes it seeks to fulfil. As with rights, however, it is clear that different sets of aims and objectives may be used to judge the effectiveness of alternative provision. These sets of aims and objectives include:

- national aims for the education system as a whole
- aims of local authority policy
- specific aims of particular types of alternative provision
- individual aims of those involved.

The overall purposes and aims of education have always been, and will always be, a matter of political debate. Legislation defines education in our society as incorporating aims about the spiritual, moral, cultural, mental and physical development of pupils. These overall aims are elucidated further in documents by which our schools are judged. Some examples are the documents setting out guidelines for the curriculum which is expected to be covered in schools, or the criteria used in inspections by the Scottish HMI (Ofsted in England and Wales). In other words, despite the political and value-laden nature of views on education, there are public documents which carry weight as standards by which schools may be judged. Basically, it is agreed that the education system should offer pupils a broad and balanced curriculum, suited to their age and aptitudes. It is also the case that the education system is expected to be accountable in terms of standards of educational attainment and school attendance (and to provide value for money).

These national standards have been used to assess the effectiveness of alternative educational provision (e.g. HMI, 1990; Ofsted, 1995). There are problems with this approach, however. One potential problem is that some aspects of the broadly defined aims of education, such as moral or spiritual development, are hard to quantify and measure in terms of outcomes. Hence, there may be a temptation to concentrate on the overall aims which produce 'hard' measurable outcomes and to value only such 'hard' outcomes as evidence of effectiveness. As Simpson (1992) and others point out, some staff working in alternative provision feel that the definition of education by which their work is judged concentrates unduly on narrow aims which can be easily measured. One criticism, then, of using national aims and objectives of education as the standard of effectiveness is that too often the judgement includes only those aspects of education which are most easily measured.

Another criticism made is that national aims and objectives may not reflect those of the particular provision being judged. This is the case, for example, if an aim of the alternative provision is to offer particular treatments or therapies. Others have gone further and argued that it is important to ask how closely any stated aims for education reflect those of all parties involved in alternative provision; that is, do such standards equate with notions of effective education in the minds of the children involved, of their parents, of the staff and of involved professionals (Cole *et al.*, 1998)? Thus, it is argued, despite the fact that nationally we have a view of effective education, it must be remembered that this may not reflect the aims and purposes of particular people involved in alternative provision.

Another rider to accepting nationally set aims and purposes as standards by which to judge effectiveness is that we know performance varies greatly depending on pupil intake. It is now established that educational performance varies enormously between disadvantaged and advantaged areas (e.g. NCE, 1996; Rodger, 1994). Thus, the effectiveness of alternative provision has to be judged according to the 'value added' to the pupils in relation to attaining these overall aims and purposes. In addition, as we argued in Chapter 3, schools can only do so much; the structural causes of educational disadvantage are ameliorated or worsened according to political decisions about social and economic policy. Thus the wider social context of advantaged and disadvantaged social groups has to be borne in mind when assessing the effectiveness of alternative provision against standards of national norms.

The subjective nature of the concept of individual 'special educational needs', including those related to social, emotional and behavioural difficulties, has been much criticised in ways which make problematic its use as a standard for judging the effectiveness of alternative provision (Galloway *et al.*, 1994; Tutt, 1984). In essence, the concern is that, given the lack of any agreed criteria for defining the 'special' nature of the needs of the children who are excluded into alternative provision, by default this group can only be defined subjectively. Further, because the 'special' nature of their needs is subjectively judged, the meeting of these may be a problematic standard by which to judge effective alternative provision.

What counts as evidence?

It has been argued that effectiveness should be judged on the basis of studies which were generalisable and which produced 'hard' objectively measurable evidence and where there was a success rate above 'spontaneous remission', that is, of over 66 per cent (Topping, 1983:11–12).

The idea of counting only evidence which is generalisable and 'hard' is rejected for a number of reasons. Firstly, in discounting the validity of subjective accounts, this argument ignores the importance of day-to-day relationships in achieving success in both 'hard' outcomes, such as attendance rates, and 'soft' outcomes, such as perceptions of improvements in behaviour or attitudes. It is not enough to know that a result occurred, it is also crucial to know why that result occurred. While large surveys can indicate overall patterns, they cannot be used on their own to explain them. This gap can only be filled by subjective accounts of day-to-day practices. Secondly, concentrating solely on 'hard' outcomes ignores the question of the effectiveness of those aspects of education which are hard to measure. As we suggested above, spiritual and moral aims of education may not be measured in hard terms, yet their importance is crucial. The development of individual attitudes to the purpose of life and individual decisions about appropriate behaviour towards others can only be discussed and assessed in subjective terms. In addition, relying exclusively on 'hard' outcomes as objective, and therefore better, evidence, ignores the subjectivity both of the collection and of the interpretation of such data. Third, it is important to bear in mind the difference between generalisable data and more subjective data to which teachers can relate their own situation. Thus, qualitative evaluation is based not on hard evidence about attendance rates or qualifications gained but upon description and interpretation, upon the context and the views of those involved (Vulliamy and Webb, 1992). We would argue that it is only by taking account of both types of evidence that a clear picture of effectiveness can be obtained.

The idea of accepting only evidence of success above 66 per cent is rejected on the grounds that 'spontaneous remission', as a concept, is flawed. It is flawed because it denies the importance of day-to-day social interactions as the context which can both create, and resolve, behaviour perceived as problematic. Behaviour takes place in a social context and is affected by the style and quality of day-to-day social interactions. As Grimshaw and Berridge (1994:133) point out, 'spontaneous remission' may more plausibly be regarded as improvement occurring as the result of support and guidance offered by parents, teachers and peers on a day-to-day basis over time. Parents and teachers will recognise the long-term nature of the effort required, day in and day out, to bring up children to behave in socially acceptable ways and to work to the best of their ability. To argue that 'a large number' of disruptive children 'stop being disruptive after a while quite irrespective of what has been done to them' (Topping, 1983:11) could be seen as a denial both of the daily efforts of parents and teachers, and of the importance of the social context in understanding behaviour. The notion of spontaneous remission derives from the literature on delinquency where the criterion of successful intervention in the past was often simply that of failure to re-offend, or in fact to be caught offending. Recidivism is rejected in current thinking as the sole criterion of success, on the grounds that it lacks sufficient precise detail and takes no account of the different aims and objectives of the programmes to which young people may be disposed (Asquith and Samuels, 1994).

Finally, it is important to remember that whatever criteria one designs for amassing the evidence by which effectiveness is to be judged, the interpretation of that evidence is always a matter of subjective, value-based, political judgement. So in the end, views on the effectiveness of alternative provision will always be based upon our views on the nature of the society which all our children inhabit now, and will inherit as their future.

The effectiveness of the range of provision

Alternative educational provision is managed by both statutory and voluntary bodies and includes independent profit-making establishments. It is found in both social work and youth work settings as well as in those belonging to education departments. Sometimes there is joint funding and management. One of the difficulties in reviewing the arguments and evidence is that much of it refers to, or derives from, one professional sector. (This means that different professional concerns underpin the notions of effectiveness. What counts as effective in a social work establishment may not be the same as in an education establishment.)

The literature demonstrates the difficulty of coming to general conclusions about the relative effectiveness of different sectors of provision. For example the complexity of the varied notions of effectiveness and the different aims and objectives articulated in different settings make it impossible to come to simple conclusions, for example, that residential schools might be more effective than day schools or vice versa. As we argued earlier varied standards of effectiveness may be judged in terms of key principles, the extent to which they achieve stated aims and objectives or the extent to which they are perceived to be effective in meeting individual needs. In practice much discussion of effectiveness refers to one or more of these standards but often not explicitly. There is a lack of clarity over the aims and objectives of alternative provision, both at establishment and at authority level.

Equally there may be confusion over the application of ideas of rights, particularly when they derive from social welfare legislation, which is not applicable to educational settings. This is perceived by some to create an inconsistency and increasingly leading to an argument for the processes of assessment and placement for alternative educational settings to be based on equivalent rights. There was considerable criticism of the notion of meeting special educational needs as a basis for evaluating effectiveness of provision and also argument for the recognition of the subjective and context specific nature of the assessment of needs.

Different views were held equally of the nature of the evidence adduced to demonstrate effectiveness and of the methods used in its collection. Some argued for the exclusive gathering of hard 'objective' data in evaluating the effectiveness of provision. Others emphasised the illuminative quality of more 'subjective' methods focusing on the complex realities of everyday life. Cole and Visser (1998) argue that in the end, effectiveness in the school for children with emotional or behavioural difficulties might depend on the aggregated success of handling a thousand small variables in a number of dimensions. There is a strong case for both quantitative and qualitative methods to be used in researching this area.

The pros and cons of alternative provision

In attempting to summarise the arguments for and against the existence of out-of-school alternative provision (see Table 7.1) we inevitably simplify the sometimes very complex discussion. These arguments themselves relate to wider debates both about education and about the rights of children in our society. For example, they belong in the wider arguments about the concept of special educational needs and integration/inclusion. There are broad questions from the debates over the purposes of schooling, for example the issue of the primacy of academic achievement and its relationship to personal and social development. There are arguments which relate to

Table 7.1. A summary of arguments for and against alternative provision

Against	For
Excluded children in alternative provision are most likely to be from disadvantaged groups. If it exists children will be categorised to fit and fill it.	Exclusion exists and so it is better to have alternative provision available.
Behaviour takes place in a context so both problems and improvements may not transfer.	It protects the safety and educational well-being of the majority of pupils (i.e. those in mainstream school).
The education in alternative settings of certain children, stereotyped in terms of class, gender, ethnicity and being 'in care', prevents reflection and improvement in the mainstream.	It benefits mainstream teachers who are freed from the difficulties of having to manage certain children and are thereby enabled to teach the rest more effectively.
Pupils perceived as having SEBD have ordinary educational needs and deserve better quality mainstream education, suited to their age and aptitudes.	In alternative provision the curriculum can be differentiated to address difficulties in learning caused by problems in mainstream.
Ways of teaching developed in alternative settings may lack credibility with mainstream teachers.	The existence of alternative provision allows staff there to develop innovative ways of handling difficult children which could be of benefit to the mainstream.
Vulnerable young people may be further disadvantaged by receiving poor quality alternative education compared with that of their peers in an adequate mainstream school.	Those mainstream schools where the curriculum for academic and/or for personal and social development is poor quality may be unsuitable for vulnerable children.
Decisions about placement in alternative provision are taken in a system which can be a confusion of education and social welfare decision-making structures.	Alternative provision can be the context for productive interprofessional working.
Decisions about placement in alternative provision are often characterised by lack of clear planning or choice and by a mismatch of needs with type of provision.	Alternative provision can provide a range of therapeutic services, too specialised to be available in mainstream. It can provide more variety for disaffected young people and respond to their interests.
Exclusion and alternative placement may confirm a constellation of other features of life, such as offending non-attendance and being 'in care'.	Some young people are making their own decision not to go to mainstream school.
Removal from peer group and from community may make it more difficult to return. Segregation is more likely to reinforce, rather than solve, any difficulties.	Alternative provision can operate on a least restrictive basis.

Pupils feel rejected and stigmatised by the mainstream school.	Children and young people may feel respite from pressure. Class sizes can be small and learning may be more supportive and less threatening.
There is a lack of clarity and purpose in the alternative sector, especially in the residential and day special schools which exist in a policy context which discourages their use.	The lives of children and young people can be addressed in a holistic way. Educational needs can be planned for in a coherent way along with personal and social needs.
Children and young people may experience problems in their social relationships in an 'abnormal' environment.	They may be able to form strong and significant relationships with supportive adults.
There is a lack of accountability in this sector. This whole range of provision continues to exist and to be used without proper evaluation.	
Alternative educational provision is used as a last resort and may, therefore, be perceived as an educational and social dustbin.	

the politics of social justice, to the discussion of ideas of advantage and disadvantage. There is not space here to address all of this but it is important to recognise that the debate over the existence or value of alternative educational provision takes place as part of wider debates which also belong in our particular social, economic and political context.

The quality of provision

Overall the literature on the quality of experience of alternative provision paints a very mixed picture. Positive views of certain kinds of provision tended to be provided more often in the writing of practitioners. Certain concerns were expressed across the whole range of provision. There was overall a critical view of the range of curriculum offered in alternative provision and of the quality of the overall educational experience of pupils and a general concern for the standard of care in residential establishments. There was a concern for the quality of peer group relationships available to pupils in alternative provision (John, 1996). This was of particular concern for girls who may be in very small numbers. The issue of gender tended to be rarely considered in the literature (Lloyd, 1999a; 1999b). There was recognition of the quality of relationships developed by pupils with staff in alternative provision and of feelings of security and safety engendered

(Cooper, 1993; Craig, 1995, Cole *et al.*, 1998; Cole and Visser, 1998). The quality of experience was often positively evaluated in comparison with previous negative experiences of mainstream school or of no education.

Evaluation of immediate outcomes in relation to objectives is more straightforward when there is clarity over aims and objectives although this clarity is not always apparent. There is general agreement that improving educational attainment is problematic (Ofsted, 1995). Evidence is mixed but on balance pupil attainment in alternative provision seems low. Local authority policy aims such as reintegration seem not to be often achieved, although there is some evidence as to how this could be improved (Normington, 1992; Stirling, 1994; Bullock *et al.*, 1994; Lloyd and Padfield, 1996). A recent UK-wide study of reintegration from schools and units for Emotional and Behavioural Difficulties found that very few pupils were being reintegrated into mainstream schools (Farrell and Tsakalidou, 1999). Resistance to reintegration from mainstream schools seems common, as is the problem of 'out of sight, out of mind' exemplified in this comment about an off-site support unit from our exclusion research.

> They are still on our school roll but we've forgotten about them and I feel that I haven't done justice to some of our children because of that. I think we have maybe given up our responsibilities in that whereas if it was based in school, we would make more of an effort to keep them and there would perhaps be more of a success rate in having them return to mainstream.
>
> (Primary teacher, Menteith School)

Preparation for life outwith the alternative provision may be an appropriate aim for some schools which at present seems to be ineffectively addressed. Individual establishments tend to rely on criteria involving evaluation of the immediate experience of pupils rather than on evidence of outcomes. Evaluation of improvement in pupils' behaviour tends to be context specific and does not include consideration of the transfer of gains to other settings. There is a lack of evidence of the views of children, young people and their parents of desirable outcomes from alternative educational placement. We believe that there is a need for an approach to the evaluation of immediate outcomes which can correlate gains in relation to multiple aims, e.g. reintegration, educational achievement, attendance and personal and social development.

There is a very limited amount of information on longer-term outcomes. Generally outcomes appear to be less favourable when compared with achievements of mainstream peers, for example, in relation to qualifications and employment. Outcomes concerning long-term personal development such as more favourable self-concept are claimed but are difficult to support from current research findings. There is an argument for further research exploration of this. There is almost no discussion of pupils' own subsequent experience of being parents. This may be important especially as there is in some of the literature a sense of repeated experience across generations and evidence of early parenthood (Kahan, 1994). Overall it is difficult to isolate key factors influencing longer-term outcomes from wider factors such as general maturation and other experiences of life, e.g. personal relationships, additional to those of the alternative educational establishment. There is still, however, a strong case for this aspect to be more widely researched.

Conclusions

The picture reflected here is not very optimistic. Much of the literature is very critical of the quality of education and care offered, of a lack of clarity over the aims and purposes of much alternative provision, and of an absence of clear evaluative criteria for looking at effectiveness. The most positive views of the various kinds of alternative provision discussed tend to come from practitioners, enthusiastic about the value of their own setting. These accounts are knowledgeable and insightful but would be more valuable if supported by evaluative studies.

We recognise that many teachers believe that pupils with difficulties in school may be better served in a more specialised setting, where it is assumed that staff will be trained and equipped to deal with challenging behaviour. There is, however, a question over the extent of such specialised training. The effectiveness of special provision is also challenged by the rising rates of exclusion from special schools (Parsons, 1999). There is also a tension in the system where alternative provision is seen simultaneously both as a way of getting rid of troublesome pupils and a haven offering more specialised support. The existence of the provision can be used as a warning or threat to pupils – 'You realise that if you don't behave you might be sent to a residential school and you wouldn't like that, would you?' – which then becomes translated into different language when the threat becomes reality – 'You are going to this school because it will really help you'. This is accompanied in many schools by a widely held, but largely inaccurate, view that difficult pupils are now all in mainstream schools and that there is little use of special provision.

The availability and use of provision is highly varied geographically. Public expenditure restrictions in the last twenty years combined with a policy emphasis on public–private partnerships led to considerable insecurity in voluntary sector provision. In our research there was a sense that some previously supportive out-of-school projects were currently under threat, as central government start-up money was not able to be continued by local councils.

> I don't know if I mentioned this before but when we were talking about behaviour cards and targeting specific trends and aspects of behaviour that we wanted to do something about, we work a lot with a group called the Family Education Support Project. Because they have the time to work on a one-to-one basis, they do a lot of this work for us and we are deeply indebted to them. They are, yet again, something that is probably going to go under this new authority.
>
> (Headteacher, primary school)

The kind of specialised support available depended hugely on where you lived. Parsons (1999) and others have identified the problem of 'projectitis' where new and innovative approaches are set up but are not sustained or incorporated into mainstream practice. Where there have been examples of successful practice in alternative provision these have often not been communicated for the benefit of mainstream teachers. Alternatively it may be that what is successful in alternative provision for pupils in difficulty may be the same strat-egies that are successful in supporting children in mainstream.

There is a clear case for more research into the effectiveness of alternative provision. This research should, as argued earlier, take account of both 'soft' and 'hard' measures of outcome. There is a need for an approach to the evaluation of immediate outcomes which can correlate gains in relation to multiple aims, e.g. reintegration, educational achievement, attendance and personal and social development, and for long-term research into the impact on the future lives of young people. There could be more discussion and research into ideas of best value and cost effectiveness in relation to aims and outcomes which could usefully be informed by the broad idea of 'production of welfare' (Knapp and Fenyo, 1994; Parsons, 1996b).

There is a sense of ambivalence at local authority level; as current policies emphasise inclusion, therefore the existence of alternative provision in a sense implies failure. The professional pragmatic response may be therefore to regard the alternative sector simply as a rather undesirable but still useful resource. There seems a strong argument for an open professional debate about the place and purposes of out-of-school provision in the current policy climate. This debate at the moment tends only to be engaged in by proponents of alternative provision. Those who favour a more inclusive approach tend to ignore the continued use of this provision on a relatively wide scale in Britain. Equally the debate must relate to the wider discussion of the aims and purposes of mainstream education and the rights of children and teachers in school. This might help us in determining more clearly the standards against which the effectiveness of alternative provision should be judged.

8

'Together to School Again'?
Perspectives on Inclusion and
Exclusion in Different Countries

We are at the beginning of an exploration of the subtle differences
of the meaning of the processes and practices of inclusion and
exclusion between different countries.

(Booth and Ainscow, 1998:246)

In this chapter we discuss the broad issues that emerge from the
research and literature of other countries, especially those with education systems facing similar challenges to Britain. We acknowledge
the limits and the possibilities of making comparisons, especially
where words like exclusion have multiple and contested meanings,
even in one language. We look at the use of disciplinary exclusion
from school in different places, at varied conceptualisations of behavioural difficulties and inclusion and at the impact of such conceptualisations on provision. The relationship of these with wider aspects
of educational and social policy debates, such as those about violence
in school, about educational 'standards' and about juvenile justice, is
recognised. Finally we consider the policy contradictions and dilemmas which contextualise the international move towards inclusion.

We draw on the literature on Western and Eastern Europe and
Australia but make particular reference to the USA. This is for two
reasons. First, there is a general tendency for British educators to 'borrow' ideas or practices from the USA. This has been, as Garner (1995)
points out, especially so in the fields of special education and educational psychology. Some commonly used terminology, such as
'mainstream' and 'inclusion', has its origins in North America.
Second, more recently there has been a strong move within the
writing on emotional and behavioural difficulties in Britain towards
the use of concepts derived from American professional, particularly
psychiatric literature (Cooper, 1999a). This is apparent, for example,

129

in the increasing widespread use of the term Attention Deficit Hyperactivity Disorder.

The limits and possibilities of comparison

We recognise the difficulties of drawing conclusions based on comparisons between different systems or indeed of assuming homogeneity within systems in each country. As the Scottish authors of this book we are particularly aware, for example, of the tendency in much academic writing on education to ignore the legislative and practice diversity within Britain (Paterson, 1997). The complexity of the comparative process is clearly summarised by Booth and Ainscow (1998). They identify the 'two pitfalls of comparative research: first that there is a single national perspective on inclusion or exclusion, and the notion that practice can be generalised across countries without attention to local contexts and meanings' (Booth and Ainscow, 1998:4). Concepts such as integration and inclusion have a meaning within the geographical and historical context of their educational system. These ideas will often not be fixed but in a dynamic process where their meanings are disputed by the participants in that system. Nonetheless the discussion of ideas and experiences from other systems does provide an opportunity to explore taken-for-granted assumptions and practices. For example, at a recent international conference at which a paper on gender and disciplinary exclusion was being presented, a European colleague interrupted to clarify what exclusion was. The notion of denying access to full-time schooling because of unacceptable behaviour was simply not recognised within his educational system.

Comparisons of rates of exclusion

It is particularly difficult to make comparisons over rates of exclusion and suspension. As with international tables of crime statistics the biggest differences may lie in the collection and organisation of the figures (Smith, 1995). However, it can still be argued that there is evidence of a substantial increase in rates of disciplinary exclusion from school in the 1980s and 1990s in Britain, the USA and Australia and a definite increase in thinking, writing and policy-making about this theme (Slee, 1995; Parsons, 1999). As has been pointed out earlier, the methods of collection of data on exclusion vary, for example between England and Scotland, and in some countries national figures are not available. In the USA, the Federal Department of Education has been concerned for some time over apparently rising rates of exclusion, partly as a consequence of the development of zero tolerance policies in schools. However, the Department does not collect national statistics, nor are these widely available in a comparable basis from individual states or indeed from school districts or schools. The terminology in the USA and Australia tends to be that of suspension and expulsion, maintaining the difference, between short-term cooling off and permanent removal from the school. This is perhaps understood more clearly by parents and children than the British language of exclusion.

These processes can be seen in different ways, for example as an element of disciplinary practice; as a stage in the identification of those who may be considered to require full-time alternative educational placements outwith the mainstream school; or as a means of putting pressure on authorities to find such a place, as exemplified in the comment quoted at the start of Chapter 6, from the headteacher in our exclusions research. 'Suspension procedures operate in concert with the increasing surveillance and regulation of students through "special needs provisions". Suspension is an influential entry in the student dossier to trigger professional interest' (Slee, 1995:56).

The possibility of some school pupils being denied access to full-time schooling for significant periods as a result of disruptive behaviour, as in the USA and in Britain, appears not to exist to the same extent in Western Europe. Parsons (1999:33–34) refers to Denmark, the Netherlands, Belgium, France, Germany, Austria, Luxembourg, Spain and the Republic of Ireland when he states that 'a *fundamental principle* in all these countries is that all children who are nationals of that country or who are resident in that country should be receiving a full-time education . . . if a child is to be expelled from school, it is the headteacher's responsibility to find another placement for the child before the exclusion occurs'. There are, however, some examples of schools in these countries excluding children for a short period of time, the regulation of this sometimes varying between regions within countries. This is the case in parts of Austria where the headteacher is allowed to exclude for one day but pupils can be excluded for up to four weeks on the decision of the local School Inspector. In Denmark a pupil may be excluded from school for a period of up to a week not more than twice in one academic year (Eurydice, 1999). Pupils in the final, non-compulsory, year of the Folkschule may be excluded permanently. In Italy exclusion is rarely used as a sanction but schools are permitted to exclude for up to five days, up to 15 days and to the end of the school year. The last option must be decided by the school board. Permanent exclusion is very rare (Eurydice, 1999). Exclusion is also rare in Finland; the minimum time of exclusion is one month and the maximum three months. The decision cannot be made by the head but must be taken by the school board. In the Netherlands, while it is possible to send a pupil home for some days, it would be expected that in-school alternatives had been explored first – a colleague from a research agency in the Netherlands said: 'What is unthinkable in the Dutch context, however, is total expulsion without arranging other educational facilities' (Walraven, G. SARDES, personal communication). This is also the case in the Czech Republic where there is no procedure for expulsion from school, although, as in Britain, headteachers may arrange to exchange or 'host' pupils who are considered to be causing problems. Such pupils may also be referred to special day or residential provision, for excluded pupils or for emotional and behavioural difficulties as in England. It may be that this course of action is more possible in those countries with relatively large numbers of places in segregated special schools. This again points to the complex relationship in Europe, the USA and in Britain between the processes of exclusion, inclusion and special education. Suspension, expulsion and exclusion can be seen in contrast with, or as a contradiction within, the major international movements towards inclusion.

Exclusion and inclusion

There is a growing international literature on inclusion. The term 'inclusion' is now more likely to be used than integration. There is a lack of clarity in the definition and usage of the terms, inclusion sometimes being used as if it refers narrowly to what is also sometimes called special education (Clark *et al.*, 1995; Reezigt and Pijl, 1998; Booth and Ainscow, 1998). The concept was originally developed in the USA (Lipsky and Gartner, 1997). The dissemination of the idea was encouraged in the rest of the world through two conferences organised by the United Nations, the second of which culminated in the Salamanca Statement, mentioned in Chapter 7. Paradoxically, successive Federal governments in the USA have taken an ambivalent view of the United Nations, shown by their reluctance to pay their dues and by the failure to acknowledge or incorporate into US law the protection to children's rights offered by the UN Convention on the Rights of the Child. However, the development of the movement towards inclusion in the USA, and in particular the growing organisation of disabled people, was very influenced by the history of the

American civil rights movement. Here it is possible to see in a clear form the contradiction which is also evident in many European and developed countries – that between the notions of rights-based group entitlement to particular forms of education, enshrined in law, and an individualised, identification and special placement model also defined in law and supported by central government funding mechanisms.

The notion of integration of children considered to have special educational needs (Britain) or disabilities (USA) into mainstream schooling originated in the literature and legislation in the 1970s and early 1980s. The Warnock report and the 1980 and 1981 Education Acts in England and Scotland, like Public Law 94-142 in the USA, represented a change in thinking which was more critical of, although not rejecting, segregated special education. The effect of this, and subsequent, legislation in the USA has been to increase substantially the numbers of pupils identified and funded as having disabilities, although the placement pattern has not altered dramatically (Lipsky and Gartner, 1997; Ware, 1998). As in Britain, the rhetoric of integration tended to obscure the continued placement of children into specialised alternative educational settings (Riddell and Brown, 1994). The proportion of children educated in segregated provision varies between countries: for example, almost 4 per cent of pupils in the Netherlands attend full-time special schools but just over 1 per cent in Scotland (Reezigt and Pijl, 1998; Closs, 1997). In Denmark 0.7 per cent of school pupils attend special schools and 1 per cent attend special classes in the mainstream. The process of reducing the numbers in segregated schools has perhaps been most problematic in countries like the Netherlands, Belgium and Germany which had highly specialised, differentiated and well funded systems of special education (Pijl and Meijer, 1991). In the Netherlands in 1995, there were 51 special schools for severe behaviour problems (Reezigt and Pijl, 1998). Concern about the proportion of children in special schools has led to the development of new procedures designed to maintain pupils in regular primary education. 'The inclusion policy is known as the "together to school again" policy, which in Dutch is: Weer Samen Naar School' (Reezigt and Pijl, 1998). However, as in many countries, it seems that this policy is most easily implemented in relation to some groups of children, whereas those whose behaviour is most challenging are still more likely to be educated in segregated settings.

Although in many countries there continues to be a segregated system of special schools, often the population of these has changed. In Britain, Australia, the USA and most of Europe there has been a move into the mainstream of pupils with physical and sensory disabilities, while this has been less likely for those with severe learning difficulties and those with emotional or behavioural difficulties. However, the literature on integration, and more recently on inclusion, often fails truly to consider the last group. In their recent collection of papers on international perspectives on inclusion, Booth and Ainscow (1998) observe that their contributors assume this concept refers to the population often associated with special education, children with physical, sensory or learning disabilities. Booth himself develops the idea of exclusion in a wider sense than disciplinary exclusion to denote a broader denial of access to education of a range of different groups such as Travellers and pregnant school-age girls, as well as pupils considered to have special educational needs (Booth, 1996).

Defining emotional and behavioural difficulties

The population of pupils described as having emotional or behavioural difficulties (England), social, emotional or behavioural difficulties (Scotland), emotional disturbance (USA) is problematic for much of the literature on inclusion. The idea, for example, of celebrating diversity is more difficult to argue than in relation, for example, to physical disability. It is also not entirely clear when a pupil whose behaviour is a problem for a school becomes a pupil with special educational needs (Britain) or disabilities (USA). The legislation tends to suggest that the difference lies in the notion of intentionality or in the individual pupil's ability to control their own behaviour. Often government advice attempts to distinguish between pupils who are 'bad' and those with psychological difficulties (DFE, 1994).

In Scotland this distinction is not maintained in official discourse, although often may be voiced in informal professional discussion. There is no official definition of social, emotional or behavioural difficulties. A Report by Inspectors of School on provision for children identified with social, emotional or behavioural difficulties recognised that it was not possible to find an agreed definition of the kind of behaviour which led to placement, that it was difficult to establish how many children were identified and that the kind of support they received was as much to do with the provision available where they lived as to do with diagnosis and assessment of need (HMI, 1990). Research into the reintegration of pupils into mainstream found that professionals tended to use very loosely terminology like maladjusted, 'EBD', disaffected, troubled, troublesome, disturbed and others without agreed definition (Lloyd and Padfield, 1996).

In the USA the law on the identification of emotional disturbance has a clause often referred to as the social maladjustment exclusion clause. This specifically rules out children regarded as socially maladjusted 'without emotional disturbance' from categorisation under the law and therefore as eligible for Federal funding for services (US Department of Education, 1998b). This leads to some inconsistent practice as students identified with 'conduct disorders' are considered ineligible for funding in some states but included in others. The US Department of Education Report to Congress on these issues (1998b) recognised that this means some students 'are provided access to therapeutic services and considered victims of their disorders . . . students who are considered antisocial or socially maladjusted are usually blamed for their aversive and maladaptive behaviour patterns and exposed to control, containment or punishment strategies' (Walker *et al.*, 1990, cited in US Department of Education, 1998 II-49). In England a similar distinction may be observed between pupils formally identified with emotional or behavioural difficulties, who may be sent to special schools, and excluded pupils, who may be sent to Pupil Referral Units set up specifically for excluded pupils.

The difficulties of sustaining this position are acknowledged by the Federal Department of Education in the USA. The Report to Congress cited above states:

> the literature also suggests that there are no valid theoretical or empirical grounds for differentiating between conduct disorders and other behavioural and emotional disorders and that there are no reliable or socially validated instruments for making such a distinction.

> (US Department of Education II-48)

Nevertheless the distinction is sustained in most of the education systems discussed in this chapter, reflecting a separation of, and creating an uneasy balance between, structures of discipline and support.

In the USA, public concern over school safety, especially in the context of school shootings, has been associated with rising exclusion rates. Recognition of the high proportion of students with identified disabilities, particularly emotional disturbance, amongst those excluded has led to new Federal requirements on schools, as specified in the Regulations associated with the recent reauthorization of IDEA, Individuals with Disabilities Education Act (Federal Register, 1999). Schools are now limited in the number of days for which they can exclude pupils who have been identified with a disability for the purpose of receiving special services – beyond ten days the school must ensure that the student is receiving an education as specified in their Individual Education Programme. However, some children identified with a disability may be regarded as responsible for their own actions:

> If the IEP team concludes that the child's behaviour was not a manifestation of the child's disability, the child can be disciplined in the same manner as non-disabled children, except that appropriate educational services must be provided. This means that if non-disabled children are long term suspended or expelled for a particular violation of school rules, the child with disabilities may also be long term suspended or expelled.
>
> (Federal Register, 1999)

It is intended that the new regulations will reduce the numbers of students on the streets. For those 'non-disabled' pupils who are considered responsible for their own actions, there is no federally prescribed protection. In some states they may be placed in an alternative educational establishment, in others they may receive no schooling.

Standards for pupils with emotional or behavioural difficulties

A common concern in several education systems focuses on the recognition of the relatively lower school achievements of pupils identified as having emotional or behavioural difficulties. In the USA, for example, in 1994 the US Department of Education published a National Agenda for Achieving Better Results for Children and Youth with Serious Emotional Disturbance. This recognised, as has also been acknowledged in Britain, that pupils identified with emotional or behavioural difficulties achieve lower academic performance, are more likely to drop out of school, to truant and to commit offences. There is concern, as discussed earlier, in particular over standards within special provision. The debate over the existence or value of educational provision for children considered to have emotional or behavioural difficulties takes place as part of wider debates over standards, over inclusion and over selection which also belong in their particular social, economic and political context. Booth and Ainscow (1998) argue that to make sense of inclusive processes *in one school* an exploration of the national political, economic, cultural and legislative contexts and their history, as well as the particular history of the school, is essential.

Gender, 'race' and ethnicity

The relationship with the structures of the wider social context is also evidenced in the disproportionality of exclusion amongst certain groups of pupils (Slee, 1995; Ofsted, 1996; Parsons, 1999) and in their representation in special provision for children considered to have emotional and behavioural difficulties. In Britain, black boys with an African Caribbean background are over five times more likely to be excluded from school and are more likely to be in special provision (Parsons, 1999). In the USA, there is current concern over the population of pupils diagnosed as having emotional disturbance. 'Within this statistically and diagnostically diverse population, females appear to be under-represented and African Americans appear to be over-represented' (US Department of Education, 1998a Section II–46). Slee (1995) cites the vulnerability to exclusion from school of Maori pupils in New Zealand and suggests that this is also the case for Aboriginal children in Australia. In Belgium and the Netherlands boys from ethnic minority families are over-represented in special education. In all the countries where there is an over-representation of children from ethnic minorities in special education this is also related to social class and poverty (US Department of Education, 1998b). In several countries in Eastern Europe, for example the Czech Republic, there is a disproportionate number of Romany children in various forms of special provision, including schools for those considered to have emotional or behavioural problems (Closs, 1996; Ainscow and Haile-Giorgis, 1998). In England, Ofsted identified a problem of disproportionate exclusion of Gypsy Traveller pupils (Ofsted, 1996). In Scotland, a recent study also found that some Gypsy Traveller pupils had been excluded and argued that this should be seen as part of a wider experience of social exclusion (Lloyd et al., 1999). Since patterns of exclusion from school mirror the wider picture of disadvantage and prejudice this suggests that exclusion from school might be viewed as a questionable practice.

Funding and labelling

The autonomy of states in the USA means that the Federal law and regulations are difficult to impose and depend on the co-operation of school districts and schools who wish to receive Federal funding. The relationship between funding and the identification of particular conditions or disabilities is an issue in many countries. In Britain, since the Education Acts of the early 1980s, funding has been associated with the identification of individual pupils with special educational needs for Statementing (England and Wales) or Recording (Scotland). The definition of SEN is not categorically based but depends on the perceived ability of the pupils to access the curriculum. However, the development of the quasi-market in education and the greater financial autonomy of schools has meant that the identification of special need is inevitably associated with structures of possible funding and there is some evidence that labelling with a particular medicalised diagnosis, for example Attention Deficit Hyperactivity Disorder, may mean that financial support is more likely (Dyson, 1997; Parsons, 1999).

Individual pupil versus whole-school approaches

Funding issues are also involved in the move, associated with developing ideas of inclusion, towards more whole-school approaches to dealing with difficult and disruptive behaviour. Often funding arrangements depend on different local and national budgets, with different criteria for funding individual responses from those for supporting wider approaches. At both state and Federal level in the USA, there is encouragement for schools to consider whole-school approaches to the prevention of violence, particularly in the context of the tragic incidents of pupil and teacher deaths at the hands of pupils with guns. In the booklet sent to all schools, well functioning schools are seen to:

- have a focus on academic achievement;
- involve families in meaningful ways;
- develop links to the community;
- emphasise positive relationships among students and staff;
- discuss safety issues openly;
- treat students with equal respect;
- create ways for students to share their concerns;
- help children feel safe expressing their feelings;
- have in place a system for referring children who are suspected of being abused or neglected;
- offer extended day programmes for children;
- promote good citizenship and character;
- identify problems and assess progress towards solutions;
- support students in making the transition to adult life and the workplace (US Department of Education, 1998a).

Schools are encouraged to collect their own data on performance on these aspects. Some states, influenced by the Federal document, and by the research into effective schools, have set up state-wide development programmes. These are supported by university staff, for example 'The Effective Schools Program' based in the Institute on Violence and Destructive Behaviour, University of Oregon. Staff from this programme have been involved in helping developments like the Montana Behavioural Initiative, 'a comprehensive staff development venture created to improve the capacities of schools and communities to meet the increasingly complex social, emotional and behavioural needs of students' (MBI, 1999). In Montana five school/community partnerships were established in different parts of the state. Each of these set up teams of school staff, parents and community representatives to identify priorities for their school. These teams were then supported by trained facilitators to develop 'positive, proactive and preventive' programmes to be implemented both in school and in the community.

In some states in the USA and in parts of Europe, including Britain, there is increasing use of specialist peripatetic support for the mainstream. This operates in both a preventive and a responsive manner as outlined below in Austria.

Ambulant teachers, specially trained for the mainstreaming and care of children with behavioural problems, work in the Viennese school system. In the school year 1997/98, 149 ambulant teachers were responsible for overseeing 4,617 children from elementary, middle and special schools. This very different approach to the role of the teacher-educator calls for the care of troubled children themselves, along with systemic counselling, conflict management, the counselling of parents as well as teachers, and includes interdisciplinary work with institutions associated with the school system. It also requires involvement in preventive efforts to avert outbreaks of asocial behaviour.

(Felsleitner, 1999)

Peripatetic systems of support may still be focused on individual children or may also provide consultancy for the development of more whole-school approaches. Both individual and systemic approaches are argued to be necessary, as alternatives to exclusion, in a monograph produced as one of a series by the influential CCBD (Council for Children with Behavioural Disorders) in the USA. 'To be proactive (i.e. positive and preventive), interventions for students with EBD must be supported and maintained by a collaborative, comprehensive and positive school-wide system of behaviour support (Gable et al., 1998:31).

Connections with juvenile justice and welfare systems

There is a clearly recognised connection in many countries between problems at school and in the community. As we have argued earlier, many children excluded from school have experienced problems in their families and may also be involved in delinquency. They may therefore be subject to formal processing and placement through other systems, for example those related to social welfare and/or juvenile justice. Such systems may also be connected with educational decision-making and may, as in the case of the Children's Hearing System in Scotland, make an important contribution to the general climate of decision-making about children. There may also, however, be tension both between professionals involved in juvenile justice, social welfare and education and between legislation relating to the different sectors. In the USA recently there was an attempt in Congress to use Federal juvenile justice legislation to undermine the restrictions on expulsion from school introduced previously in educational law and regulations (IDEA, 1997). In Britain, the Children Acts in England (1989) and in Scotland (1995), which recognise in law the rights of children as outlined in the UN Convention, do not apply in education but only in reference to the social welfare of children.

A report commissioned by the Scottish Executive on the international context of juvenile justice argued that, while most national systems of dealing with children and young people in trouble contain elements of both welfare and justice, the balance has recently changed (Hallett and Hazel, 1998). Concern for the rights of juveniles in proceedings relating to them has increased along with a greater separation (although not in Scotland) between decision-making over offending and that over more general welfare concerns. In the USA and in England, there has been a greater emphasis on deterrence, punishment and incarceration. 'Scotland's Children's Hearings System has proved largely immune from developments on conservative crime control and polarisation of severity by making little formal distinction in principle between offenders and children in need of care and protection and by excluding overtly punitive disposals' (Hallett and Hazel, 1998:iii). In Scotland, decision-making over exclusion from school, although resting formally with the headteacher, in practice often includes discussion at an inter-agency meeting, sometimes called a school liaison group or a joint assessment team. Such groups were set up in most Scottish councils as part of Youth Strategies aimed at promoting inter-agency collaboration and reducing the numbers of children excluded from school and placed away from their family and community. The Family Group Conferences in New Zealand have some aspects in common with the Scottish Children's Hearings in that they stress mediation between family and community and try to divert children away from formal court proceedings. A number of experimental schemes based on the New Zealand model are being tried in England.

There has been a general discussion in Europe over the use of residential placement for delinquent young people and in many countries a policy of reduction of their incarceration, although secure provision remains a key aspect of provision, for example in Britain (Littlewood, 1996). In most European countries there is a point where a balance is struck between welfare and punitive approaches, sometimes relating to age and sometimes to a professional judgement as to whether an offence is to be seen as a sign of a welfare problem (Walgrave, 1996). In some states in the USA there has been a reduction of the age of referral to adult courts leading to more longer and more stringent, particularly custodial, sentences (Hallett and Hazel, 1998). As in special educational provision and in exclusion processes, there is in many countries concern over the over-representation of boys and of young people from some ethnic minorities. In Australia, for example, Aboriginal children form 4.4 per cent of the juvenile population and 70 per cent of those in detention.

Another identifiable trend in terms of social welfare has been the dramatically increased numbers of children identified as experiencing child abuse. In Scotland the Reporters to the Children's Hearings find this increasingly occupies their time. Between 1985 and 1994 there was an increase of 300 per cent in the numbers of children referred on grounds of abuse or neglect. Hallett and Hazel (1998) and others talk of the rediscovery of child abuse as a social problem. They also quote figures from the US Department of Health and Human Services which show more than a million children identified as victims of abuse or neglect. In many countries systems of child protection form part of an administrative system of social welfare, increasingly separated in most English speaking countries (Scotland is an exception) from systems dealing with juvenile justice systems. Many of the European countries still have more unified systems (Hallett and Hazel, 1998). Child protection procedures have been identified in several countries as a particular challenge to, and as an argument for, effective interprofessional working. This was identified for example in the Report of the Inquiry into the removal of children from Orkney in Scotland (Tisdall, 1996). If abuse and delinquency are seen to be related to the experience of exclusion from school then there are questions about the separateness in many countries of the systems set up to respond to each of these. Developments in juvenile justice and in social welfare are clearly related to, and can have a direct impact on, inter-professional working in relation to exclusion from school.

Summary of common issues and themes

Diversity of opinion within countries is inevitably reflected in the literature which sometimes presents quite different views from the same system. In Booth and Ainscow's collection of comparative papers Bailey describes Australia as 'highly centralised' (1998:173) whereas the editors, commenting on his paper, quote the view of Ward (1993) who argues that as far as special education is concerned, at least, the Australian states present a 'bewildering diversity of philosophies and practices' (Ward, 1993:135, quoted by Booth and Ainscow, 1998). Bailey also describes a commitment to the principles of inclusive education, for example in the state of Queensland, whereas Slee (1995) sees the dividing practices of special education reappearing in the guise of inclusive education. Slee also sees the development of practices of suspension in Australia in the context of the abolition of corporal punishment and the associated development of discipline policies. (Corporal punishment, no longer used in state schools in Europe, is still a feature of educational systems in many parts of the world, for example in some American states. US law also allows the use of chemical and physical restraints of pupils with emotional or behavioural difficulties which would be illegal in Britain.)

Common to many education systems is a growing concern about school discipline/violence. As we have argued in this chapter, this is expressed in a number of countries, particularly Britain and the USA, in increasing numbers of children excluded/expelled from school. At the same time there is an international move towards a commitment to inclusion, however defined. There is widespread concern in many countries about rapidly increasing spending on special education provision, in and out of the mainstream. The emphasis on whole-school approaches to inclusion is often developing alongside and in tension with funding models which depend on individualised definitions of need. There is a lack of clarity in the literature in definitions of emotional and behavioural difficulties – the definitions inevitably reflect both social context and individual subjective perception. The acknowledgement of this subjectivity does not deny the reality of behaviour experienced by either pupils or teachers but does indicate a professional discourse characterised by semantic problems (Galloway et al., 1994; Lloyd-Smith and Dwyfor Davies, 1995; Cooper, 1999a).

Different terminology sometimes reflects different professional perspectives in their own context; for example the child who is seen to have mental health problems or psychosocial disorders in the clinic may be described in terms of Emotional or Behavioural Difficulties or emotional disturbance when at school, be delinquent and at risk in the social services context and have Special Educational Needs in terms of education law. These labels tell us as much about the formal processes of help offered to the child as they do about the child him or herself. A number of countries are recognising the need for what is often called currently in Britain 'joined up thinking' although sometimes, as argued earlier, approaches to inclusion in school may be seen to be in opposition to more punitive juvenile justice policies or to highly medicalised approaches. Parsons (1999) cites Scandinavian models of schools where he argues there is a more developed welfare-based, integrated approach. In Denmark a special project was commissioned in 1997 in which municipalities were encouraged to set up 'unruliness networks' to promote inter-agency working. In the Netherlands several cities are also experimenting with an integrated service model of school (Eurydice, 1999). In Scotland there is currently a large-scale trial of the US notion of the full service school (called in Scotland New Community schools), which are intended to embody welfare principles and provide a 'one-stop' location for pupils in need.

There is some acknowledgement of the lack of agreed criteria in defining and identifying emotional or behavioural difficulties/emotional disturbance and increasing recognition of the subjectivity of diagnosis. At the same time, there is a reaffirmation of a more medicalised approach, especially in relation to Attention Deficit Hyperactivity Disorder where the US terminology and patterns of diagnosis and drug prescription are becoming more evident in other countries, particularly in Australia and increasingly in Britain. In the USA and some European countries, especially Eastern Europe, there is much more use in education of psychiatric terminology. Also common to many countries is the uneasy tension in educational writing and policy between the notions of 'deliberate' bad behaviour and 'because of problems, genuine emotional disturbance'.

There is concern expressed in many countries among some groups of teachers and parents about categorising/labelling of children but funding still often depends on this. Equally, there is a trend towards thinking in terms of whole-school approaches but it may be difficult to get funding for whole-school approaches, although central government schemes like the Promoting Positive Discipline and Alternatives to Exclusions programmes in recent years in Scotland have encouraged this. There is an over-representation of boys and children from some ethnic minorities among those subject to disciplinary exclusion from school and in special provision for emotional or behavioural difficulties. There is a widespread lack of consideration of the experience of girls. In Britain and the USA there are considerable local variations in identification rates, provision and placement of pupils with difficulties.

Within different countries, indeed within individual schools, there are disagreements over the effectiveness or value of inclusion (Clark *et al.*, 1999). In Britain writing about exclusion from school often contextualises this as part of a wider social exclusion, related to inequality and poverty (Parsons, 1999). The arguments over inclusion and exclusion in the USA are less often related to wider issues of social inequality. In the more privatised society of the USA health insurance plays a key part in influencing provision for children considered to have mental health problems. There is a much larger private sector of residential schools and provision for children in difficulty than in European countries. Inter-professional working in Britain is, however, moving closer in style to the US model with the development of internal markets in public services and the purchaser–provider model of relationships between public and voluntary sectors.

In Western Europe the discussion of issues of exclusion and inclusion tends to refer more often than in the USA to a rights-based model, related to the UN Convention on the Rights of the Child. In the USA physical punishment continues to be used in some states and some schools. In the European Union there was a ruling that prevents its use in publicly funded schools. In the USA physical and chemical restraints are also relatively widely used in mental health provision for adolescents. In all parts of the developed world there is increasing use of pharmacological intervention with children seen to have behaviour problems, particularly, as stated earlier, in relation to the diagnosis of Attention Deficit Hyperactivity Disorder. Concerns have been expressed by the International Narcotics Control Board about the levels of prescription of methylphenidate hydrochloride in the USA (Lloyd and Norris, 1999).

In many countries there are public and professional arguments over the issue of standards and school effectiveness and improvement. These relate to arguments, in various countries, over the purposes of schooling, for example the issue of the primacy of academic achievement and its relationship to personal and social development.

The standards movement was born with good intentions. Seen in its best light, it offers the impetus for educators to infuse opportunities for all students to learn for understanding, into every aspect of school life. At its worst, it reinforces practices that our best educators know to be ineffective routes to real learning.

(Wheelock, 1999)

In this chapter it has not been possible to provide a complete account of the context of the practice of exclusion and alternatives in different countries. We believe that it has been possible to identify some themes which can be seen to be exemplified in different ways in various countries and which impact on the process of exclusion. These include broad arguments about the nature and purposes of education, about the understanding and definitions of deviance in school and in the community, about the role of special provision and movements towards reducing segregated placement. Issues of inclusion and exclusion are widely discussed in the context of an increased emphasis on educational performance. It is clear that in most countries the concept of inclusion is multiply defined and the meaning often contested.

The title of this chapter, together to school again, reflects an international movement towards greater inclusion into school of children who were traditionally excluded from participation in the mainstream. This contrasts with the increased rates in some countries of suspension, expulsion and exclusion. Clark and colleagues (1999) talk of the contrary imperatives within mass education systems and argue that the movement towards inclusion is likely to be complex and inconsistent. This tension between inclusion and exclusion from school is paralleled by that between welfare and punishment in juvenile justice systems. Equally in many countries in both education and welfare/justice systems there are definitions of worthiness and unworthiness which influence decisions made about individual children and young people. There are conflicting pressures in many countries, particularly visible in England, Scotland and USA, towards both inclusion into, and exclusion from, school and society.

9

Towards Zero Exclusion?

The ideal model would be non exclusion but . . .
(Special educational needs co-ordinator,
quoted in Kinder *et al.*, 1999a)

This book has focused on a range of alternatives to exclusion, most of which concern strategies mainstream schools can adopt to sustain young people in the school community. Chapter 7 considered alternatives to exclusion outside mainstream schools while Chapter 8 reminded us that some countries do not use exclusion as a sanction. In the debate about whether exclusion should continue to be used in the UK two issues are frequently conflated. These are, firstly, whether mainstream schools should educate *all* children and, secondly, whether exclusion should continue to be used as a sanction for disaffected behaviour. These two issues are logically quite independent. One might believe that mainstream schools cannot educate all children and yet not support the use of exclusion as a sanction. Many children are educated in specialist provision of one sort or another without having been excluded from school. Specialist provision includes, for example, those for some young people with severe and complex learning difficulties or with life threatening conditions or young people with special abilities in the arts. Thus one needs to separate arguments about the existence of different kinds of schools from the use of exclusion to punish misbehaviour.

Exclusion as punishment

Recent surveys of teacher perceptions of the nature and extent of indiscipline (Munn, Johnstone and Sharp, 1998) and on exclusion (Cullen *et al.*, 1996; Kinder *et al.*, 1999a) paint a rather complicated picture of the effectiveness of exclusion as a punishment. Some 9 per cent of Scottish secondary teachers and 3 per cent of Scottish primary teachers sampled cited 'requesting a pupil's exclusion from school' as an action they used in a particular week to deal with indiscipline in their classrooms. Yet opinion was divided about the effectiveness of this action. Nine per cent of those who had requested an exclusion saw this as their *least* effective action, while 13 per cent of secondary and no primary teachers saw it as their *most* effective action. We may infer that perceptions of effectiveness were not related to whether teachers' requests were accepted or denied by their headteachers but rather to a failure to bring about the desired changes in pupil behaviour (Munn, Johnstone and Sharp, 1998). Indeed the survey revealed that substantial percentages of both primary and secondary teachers used a number of routine actions in response to indiscipline which they perceived as ineffective, such as issuing punishment exercises or giving extra work. The data suggested that teachers were using a range of strategies from their repertoire depending on the context but with some degree of uncertainty as to their effectiveness. Furthermore, the Scottish research on exclusions (Cullen *et al.*, 1996) suggested that exclusion was not mainly for the benefit of the disruptive pupil, but rather to protect the safety of other pupils and staff and to avoid the disruption in learning for other pupils. Similar reasons for retaining permanent exclusions were given to Kinder *et al.* (1999) in their survey of 98 senior school managers in England, although the need to punish bad behaviour via exclusion was the most often cited reason (by 43 per cent of the sample), compared with 36 per cent identifying safety and other welfare reasons).

In a narrow sense permanent exclusion is an effective punishment at least from the teacher's perspective. The pupils perceived as causing problems are removed and teachers and other children can continue with their work. The impact of permanent exclusion upon the generality of pupils is more difficult to gauge. We might speculate that exclusion sends messages about the kind of behaviour which would not be tolerated in school, reinforcing the existence of the unequal power relationship between teachers and pupils and the nature of the implied contract between them. More subtly, perhaps, in terms of socialisation, exclusion is sending messages about the nature of communities, their shared assumptive worlds of norms and values as a defining characteristic and, as far as schools are concerned, the importance of conforming to norms and values. A sense of belonging is thus premised on being alike and conforming rather than on understanding or living with difference. Clearly there are some kinds of behaviour such as violence towards pupils and teachers where the immediate need is the safety of all concerned and this is the paramount duty of the school. Beyond this, however, we need to reconsider the notion of community we see schools as invoking. Fielding (1999:9) sums this up as follows: 'we need an account of community that addresses issues of diversity and difference, acknowledging the capacity of community as a form of human association to be suffocating, inward and exclusive as much as to be life-giving, outward looking and inclusive'. In considering the use of exclusion as punishment, therefore, schools are inevitably drawn into deep issues concerning their ethos and the kinds of communities they are trying to develop.

More pragmatically, the use of permanent exclusion is a very crude signal of a school's inability to meet the rights of a young person to an education. As Chapter 5 suggested, there are many strategies available to schools to support young people in trouble and we know from research that many exclusions are the culmination of a number of indications that all is not well (see Chapter 1) rather than the single dramatic incident so beloved by the media. Thus a policy of zero exclusions would need to have a series of steps and procedures worked out between the school, parents, local authority and other agencies to ensure that increasingly intensive support was available to a young person in trouble. In cases of single dramatic incidents where the safety of others is threatened then clearly steps have to be taken to protect the school community. In such cases, we would argue, there can be the need for police involvement and due process of the law.

As far as temporary exclusion is concerned, similar arguments apply. A wide range of sanctions is available to schools. 'Time out' or 'cooling off' rooms in schools used sparingly can fulfil the same function as a short-term exclusion, giving the pupil time to calm down, reflect on his or her behaviour, and consider events. Again a clearly established behaviour policy should contain support strategies for pupils in trouble and measures designed to elicit the reasons for troubled behaviour as well as describing sanctions and rewards.

As Chapter 1 made clear, exclusion can have dire consequences for young people and their families. It can engender or intensify feelings of low self-esteem, stupidity and lack of worth in young people and place additional stress and strain on families already finding it difficult to cope. A severe punishment indeed! Moreover the financial and social costs of exclusion are high. Kinder *et al.* (1999:9) report that: 'replacement education for excluded pupils is more than twice the cost of mainstream education'.

Parson's study for the Commission for Racial Equality (1996) attempted to identify social work, health and police costs of a small sample of excluded pupils as well as education costs. In his sample 20 per cent of permanently excluded pupils used social services costing on average £1,100; 10 per cent used health service resources at an average of £100; and more than 25 per cent incurred a cost to the police of an average over £2,000 (1994/95 prices). He gives the example of one young person who incurred costs to social services of £39,000 including the cost of a place in a residential school and £22,000 to the police and criminal justice system (Commission for Racial Equality, 1996:30). The Audit Commission (1996) reported that 42 per cent of young offenders had previously been excluded from school. While it would be simplistic to argue that zero exclusions would have a direct impact on crime levels, zero exclusion accompanied by high quality educational provision can help promote a sense of self-worth, increase the likelihood of achieving qualifications and hence employment which in turn reduces the risk of offending. In our view then, exclusion as a punishment is a rather blunt instrument in dealing with disaffected behaviour. It certainly provides respite for teachers and pupils but we would argue that this can be achieved in other ways. A more effective approach is one which intensifies support, provides expert analysis of the reasons for disruptive behaviour and identifies strategies for overcoming such behaviour. Implementing such policies would not be cheap but it is likely to be more cost-effective than policies which inadvertently or not encourage schools to exclude increasing numbers of young people.

Schooling for all?

Exclusion inevitably raises questions about whether mainstream schools should provide for all children and the extent to which there should be different kinds of schools (for different kinds of children). Focusing on the issue of specialist provision for children who have been permanently excluded or who have encountered a succession of fixed term exclusions raises questions about the nature of the behaviour resulting in exclusion, about the nature of the specialist provision available and about reintegration from such provision into mainstream schools.

Chapter 6 illustrated the slipperiness of the concept of social, emotional and behavioural difficulties and highlighted the wide range of behaviours and the factors underlying such behaviours which carry the label 'difficult'. Chapters 4 and 5 suggested that a school's ethos and the support it had in place for pupils and teachers helped to explain different rates of exclusion in schools with similar pupil populations. Thus the identification of behaviours resulting in exclusion and matching these to specialist provision is by no means straightforward, objective or scientific. This is well documented. In short there is not a clearly defined pupil population in need of separate specialist provision. The existence of separate provision of any kind raises questions about how children are to be allocated to it. It assumes that children are the problem and encourages a view of mainstream schools as having no responsibility for promoting or sustaining acceptable behaviour. There are echoes here of the 1930s and 1940s view of intelligence as innate and fixed, which led to the development of the Intelligence Test and to the placing of children in secondary modern or grammar schools according to their performance on a supposedly scientific and now widely discredited test. Just as Newsom (1963:6) was able to attest that 'Intellectual talent is not a fixed quantity with which we have to work, but a variable that can be modified by social policy and educational approaches', so we are slowly beginning to recognise that behaviour is not fixed, innate and immutable. Such recognition raises questions about the need for separate specialist educational provision for troubled children.

The effectiveness of specialist provision was the focus of Chapter 7. That chapter drew attention to a range of ways of conceptualising effectiveness and to the lack of systematic and rigorous evaluation of the effectiveness, however conceptualised, of specialist provision. It also highlighted the difficulties in offering a broad and balanced curriculum in such provision. The picture presented by Chapter 7 and by the range of research cited in it is not very optimistic. Criticisms abound of the quality of education and care offered, of the lack of clarity over the aims and purposes of much specialist provision and of a lack of clear evaluative criteria for effectiveness. As mentioned in Chapter 7, the most positive views of alternative provision tend to come from practitioners, enthusiastic about the value of their own setting. There is undoubtedly much dedicated work taking place and examples are given, such as that in Lewisham, of Pupil Referral Units working with mainstream schools both to support pupils in danger of exclusion and to work with pupils, parents and school staff to effect reintegration to mainstream once a pupil has been excluded (DfEE, 10/99).

We still lack a UK-wide audit of the use of full-time alternative educational provision, in public, private and voluntary sectors, including provision in social work and youth work centres. The diversity of such provision in terms of accountability procedures, management arrangements, funding and much else makes it difficult to conceptualise as a sector. Furthermore we know from studies of the characteristics of excluded pupils that the pupils in such provision are likely to consist of those already socially and economically disadvantaged. (See Chapter 1.) Providing such pupils with alternative schooling is likely to ratchet up the spiral of disadvantage. Indeed the very existence of such provision stands as a rebuke to mainstream schools' claim to be comprehensive. Clearly, if comprehensive schools are to live up to their intention to provide education for all children they need to be adequately resourced with well trained and professionally qualified staff. Too often pastoral care and behaviour support staff are catapulted into positions of responsibility affecting the care and well being of young people without adequate training. A policy designed to reduce exclusion needs to contain provision for mandatory training of such specialist staff. In addition all teachers should update their knowledge of and skills in behaviour management as part of their continuing professional development. There is now a substantial body of knowledge and a wide range of materials available in this area including examples of good practice in schools supported by their (local) education authority. There is a need to disseminate such material systematically and to relate it to staff development programmes as a matter of course.

Chapter 7 also pointed out that rates of reintegration into mainstream school for those in full-time alternative provision were low and all the disadvantages of such provision in terms of curriculum access and the gaining of educational qualifications have already been highlighted. This points to the need to use such alternative provision very, very sparingly and to have decision-making structures in place at local authority level which ensures that this is so. Barr (1994) gives an account of one authority's attempt to do this and the decline in special school placements which resulted. Chapter 7 also suggested that pupils attending part-time on- or off-site specialist provision are more easily reintegrated into mainstream schools.

Schools and society

This book has emphasised alternatives to exclusion by focusing on strategies which schools can adopt. Schools do not operate in a vacuum, although the nature of the relationships between schools on the one hand and social, economic and political structures on the other has long been a matter of debate. They have been thrown into sharp contemporary focus by the current Labour government's policy priority of 'education, education, education' as the means by which individuals will prosper, a competitive economy will be sustained and social inclusion will be promoted. Hodgson and Spours (1999:10) sum up the policy as follows:

> New Labour argues that investment in knowledge and skills will provide the essential foundation of both individual employability and the competitiveness of an economy based on high value-added goods and services which are tradable in the global market place. Second, labour market flexibility will ensure that the British economy can create jobs on a sufficient scale to tackle social exclusion. Finally, reform of the welfare state is necessary to ensure that welfare provision becomes a springboard back to work.

Policies which embody a vision of the prime job of schools as directly influencing economic and thus social relations are hardly new in mainstream British politics. The need for an educated, flexible workforce so that Britain can compete successfully with other advanced economies in the world runs through the rhetoric of both Labour and Conservative parties at least since the Second World War. What is new is the 'maximalist' notion of equality of opportunity promoted by New Labour. In essence the strategy is to provide 'recurrent equality of opportunity for individuals to learn and earn throughout their lives' (Hodgson and Spours, 1999:11) but also to ensure that a firm foundation for lifelong learning is provided by schools and grasped by young people. Thus exclusion from school, by denying the very opportunity to learn, has to be curtailed and, if possible, prevented.

In pointing up the connections between education and life chances, politicians are traversing ground well trampled by Marxist or quasi Marxist sociologists. Althusser (1971), Bowles and Gintis (1976), Bourdieu and Passeron (1977) and Bernstein (1977) set out to explain how the (more or less) direct reproduction of class relations takes place in the daily life of schools and classrooms. Rather than seeing education as the engine driving economic and social relations, however, these theorists argue that schooling serves to reproduce the social relations of production. It does so not only by determining what counts as really useful knowledge via the formal curriculum, but also by instilling values such as respect for authority and obedience and by giving pupils a sense of their own worth. Althusser, for example, suggests:

> Children at school also learn the 'rules' of good behaviour, i.e. the attitude that should be observed by every agent in the division of

labour according to the job he is destined for: rules of morality, civic and professional conscience, which actually means rules of respect for the socio-technical division of labour and ultimately the rules of the order established by class domination.

(Althusser, 1971:245, quoted in Hargreaves, 1980:175)

Hargreaves (1980) summarises the main criticisms of Althusser's model of schooling, i.e. a direct reproduction of capitalist social and economic relations, as being overly deterministic. Teachers and pupils are seen as passive, helpless and unable to resist the roles in which they have been cast. In brief, there is little attempt to explain how direct reproduction of class relations takes place and no empirical evidence of daily life in schools and classrooms to underpin his theory. Where empirical evidence has been provided as in the case of Bowles and Gintis (1976) it tends to mask the subtlety and dilemmas of relations among and between pupils and teachers. There is no account, for instance, of anti-school sub cultures which may equip pupils with strategies to resist dominant ideologies outside school.

The continuing work to develop the sociological imagination (Mills, 1959) in which the connections between private troubles and broader social structures are made explicit uses ideas of cultural, and more recently social, capital (Baron *et al.*, forthcoming; Gamarnikov and Green, 1999). Bourdieu (1986 in Halsey *et al.*, 1997:47) sums up cultural capital as follows:

Cultural capital can exist in three forms: in the *embodied* state, i.e. in the form of long lasting dispositions of the mind and body; in the *objectified* state, in the form of cultural goods (pictures, books, dictionaries, instruments, machines etc) . . . and in the *institutional* state, a form of objectification. [original emphasis]

Bourdieu in the same article (p. 47) goes on to explain that the notion of cultural capital:

initially presented itself to me, in the course of research, as a theoretical hypothesis which made it possible to explain the unequal scholastic achievement of children from different social classes by relating academic success . . . to the distribution of cultural capital between the classes and class factions. This starting point implies a break with the presupposition . . . which sees academic success or failure as an effect of natural aptitudes.

Thus Bourdieu is arguing that children who come to school predisposed to value education and who have resources at home to help them learn have inherent advantages over those without such cultural capital in terms of gaining educational qualifications and hence entry to higher education and the labour market. We have already seen, in Chapter 1, that the cultural capital with which most excluded children come to school does little to advantage them in gaining educational qualifications.

Bourdieu (1986 in Halsey *et al.*, 1997) goes on to develop the concept of social capital to explain the reproduction of elites. The American sociologist James Coleman (1988 in Halsey *et al.*, 1997) uses the concept to explain the higher than expected attainment by poor children in Catholic schools. While cultural capital is a property of individuals, social capital 'inheres in the structure of relations between actors and among actors' (Coleman in Halsey *et al.*, 1997:82). It is a resource which people (or institutions) can use to gain advantage. Portes (1998:6) describes it thus:

> [Social capital] stands for the ability of actors to secure benefits by virtue of membership in social networks or other social structures.

By using the concept to help explain underachievement and the school's role in the reproduction of social inequality, Bourdieu and Coleman direct attention to the *instrumental* role which social capital can play. The benefits or resources obtained relate to learning that will result in certification and a positional good. For example, a child unable to do mathematics homework can turn to parents to help who in turn may approach friends if they themselves cannot help with the mathematics. Similarly a school might seek to develop peer tutoring or after-school homework clubs to promote learning through the stimulation of networks of children or of adults and children. We might indeed assume that such actions on the school's part would be especially beneficial to children (actors) who did not have access to such social capital. The benefits accrue both to the individual, in terms of facilitating achievement, and to the familial network which can be seen as consolidating its broader social and economic advantage. Benefit also accrues to the school in this formulation. The more it can help children achieve, the higher up performance tables it will move, achieving local and perhaps even national approbation. It might also secure additional funding as more parents choose to send their children there as its reputation for facilitating achievement grows. Bourdieu and Coleman's starting point also draws attention to the *positive effects* of social capital. As Portes (1998) and Gamarnikov and Green (1997) point out, however, social capital can be used for undesirable ends, ranging in the school context from exclusion of outsiders, a common form of bullying (Mellor, 1999; Smith *et al.*, 1999) to networks which reinforce resistance to schools, exemplified by truanting or violence towards pupils who comply with school norms and standards (Munn, 1999a).

For a government committed to investing in equality of opportunity, however, the positive and instrumental role of social capital may prove attractive. For example, a route to developing alternatives to exclusion so that pupils become integrated with mainstream peers who provide positive role models could be to ensure that alternatives which seek to build social capital are supported.

One kind of alternative to exclusion that seeks to build social capital is the KWESI project in Birmingham. This project is run by black men and provides mentoring support for African-Caribbean boys. The project has seen exclusion rates falling by 23 per cent with two-thirds of the reduction comprising ethnic minority pupils (Social Exclusion Unit, 1998; Osler and Hill, 1999). Although not conceptualised explicitly in terms of building social capital, the project can be seen as attempting to provide a source of benefits (emotional and perhaps employment related to African-Caribbean boys) through extra familial networks which in turn begins to impact on the social control function of networks. Similarly 'Buddy systems', whereby older pupils befriend i) younger pupils transferring from nursery to primary or ii) primary to secondary schools or iii) other pupils new to the school, can be seen as a strategy to extend the network of the new pupil(s) and to secure the benefit of more rapid induction into the school's norms, values and disciplinary codes than would otherwise be the case. Such strategies can help to prevent bullying and promote compliance with school rules (Munn, 1999b).

More generally the extent to which alternatives to exclusion from school seek to promote open or closed networks among pupils within mainstream schools could be a variable explaining their success. As previously indicated, a common alternative to exclusion is the provision of a unit or base within the school to meet the needs of disaffected pupils. Units vary as to their purpose, size, the way in which pupils are allocated and the ways in which staff are recruited. A hypothesis would be that those units which sought to extend pupils' networks outwith the unit and set out to demonstrate the advantages of such networks, would be more successful in reducing the use of the unit (other things being equal) than units which did not attempt to build networks at all or confined them to regular pupil users of the unit. Such a closed network might produce a sense of social solidarity within the group but also risk the development and maintenance of a culture resistant to attainment. Such a hypothesis awaits testing empirically, although many studies of units and bases have found pupils referred to them as socially marginalised and the lack of re-integration into mainstream of pupils in off-site special units is well documented (e.g. Gray and Noakes, 1993; Ofsted, 1995; Kinder and Wilkin, 1998). Michael N.'s attempt, described in Chapter 1, to avoid his former friends and play football at break could be interpreted as trying to build new networks to secure support in his determination to 'do well' at school. Furthermore, the promotion of open networks links to the issue of sociability mentioned in Chapter 3. A justifica-tion of separate provision for disaffected pupils is the collective wel-fare of the majority of pupils in mainstream schools. They need to feel safe, secure and avoid distractions from learning which troubled young people can engender. This seems common sense. Nevertheless, separate provision may insulate the generality of pupils from a sense of social responsibility for the excluded and send a message that dif-ference is best handled via rejection. The notion of social capital encourages empirical exploration also of this kind of hypothesis.

The usefulness of the concept of social capital in understanding the effectiveness of alternatives to exclusion should not exclude other explanations, of course. This book has highlighted the importance of:

- Ideology – teachers' beliefs about the purpose of schooling and the kind of pupil they are willing to teach.
- Teachers' perceptions of the cause of learning and behaviour dif-ficulties, distinguishing 'real' difficulties from those which pupils had brought upon themselves. The former were 'worthy' and the latter 'unworthy' pupils.
- The curriculum on offer in terms of flexibility and differentiation to meet pupils' needs.
- Decision-making structures in the school, particularly the links between pastoral care systems and discipline systems.
- The school's readiness to work with outside agencies in a gen-uinely collaborative way.
- Headteachers' perceptions of the commitment of parents of excluded pupils to work with the school.
- Notions of appropriate behaviour in terms of gender and eth-nicity as well as social class.

Schools in a mass education system have to cope with a number of seemingly contradictory imperatives, some of which were described in Chapter 3. These might be summed up as 'academic standards' or pupil welfare, collective or individual rights, consistency in discipline standards or teacher autonomy, curriculum entitlement or flexibility.

There are signs in Scotland, via the first educational legislation to be developed by the Parliament, that some of these contradictory imperatives are being recognised. Politicians are anxious to convince parents, teachers and others that children's well being and happiness are as important as their cognitive-intellectual development and that there is no necessary contradiction between them. Perhaps even more important is the commitment to an anti-poverty strategy and the promise to reduce the numbers of children living in poverty. To paraphrase Levin and Kelley (1994, in Halsey *et al.*, 1997) schools can't do it alone. They argue:

> Education can work to improve productivity only if there are employment opportunities for more productive workers ... Only if education translates into opportunities which can reduce the need for welfare dependency or the incentives for criminal activity, can education be effective in diminishing these outcomes.
>
> (Levin and Kelley, 1994:240)

While it might be argued that Levin and Kelley underestimate the potency of individual agency, we can see the attractions for politicians in intervening in schooling. Schools are more controllable than the economy in this era of 'globalisation' where financial capital can move about freely and rapidly. The basic premise of this book is that there are strategies which schools can adopt to minimise exclusion. Indeed we might in time come to see exclusion as outmoded, dysfunctional and as destructive of human relations as corporal punishment. Nevertheless the move towards zero exclusion would be encouraged in a society which reduced poverty levels, provided increased employment opportunities and provided decent housing in attractive environments. The job of schools in such circumstances would be less difficult than it is currently. These conditions are all within the compass of a *determined* government; just as *determined* schools will not exclude pupils but provide good quality educational and social alternatives.

References

Abbotts, P. and Parsons, C. (1993) Children's rights and exclusion from primary school, *Therapeutic Care and Education*, Vol. 2, no. 2, pp. 416–421.

Ainscow, M. and Haile-Giorgis, M. (1998) Educational arrangements for children categorised as having special needs in Central and Eastern Europe, *European Journal of Special Needs Education*, Vol. 14, no. 2, pp. 103–121.

Allan, J., Brown, S. and Riddell, S. (1995) *Special Educational Needs Provision in Mainstream and Special Schools in Scotland*, University of Stirling.

Althusser, L. (1971) Ideology and ideological state apparatus, in L. Althusser, *Lenin, Philosophy and Other Essays*, New Left Books, London.

Anderson, V. and Merrett, F. (1997) The use of correspondence training in improving the in-class behaviour of very troublesome secondary school children, *Educational Psychology*, Vol. 17, no. 3, pp. 313–328.

Armstrong, D. and Galloway, D. (1994) Special educational needs and problem behaviour, making policy in the classroom, in S. Riddell and S. Brown (eds.) *Special Educational Needs Policy in the 90's*, Routledge, London.

Ashford, P. (1994) Who is excluded from school? Does family status have an influence, *Pastoral Care in Education*, Vol. 12, no. 4, pp. 10–11.

Asquith, S. and Samuels, E. (1994) *Criminal Justice and Related Services for Young Adult Offenders*, HMSO, Edinburgh.

Audit Commission (1996) *Misspent Youth, Young People and Crime*, Audit Commission, London.

Ayers, H., Clarke, D. and Murray, A. (1995) *Perspectives on Behaviour, A Practical Guide to Effective Interventions for Teachers*, David Fulton, London.

Bailey, J. (1998) Australia: inclusion through categorisation? in T. Booth and M. Ainscow, *From Them to Us*, Routledge, London.

Barber, M. (1996) *The Learning Game, Arguments for an Education Revolution*, Victor Gollancz, London.

Baron, S., Field, J. and Schuller, T. (eds.) (forthcoming) *Social Capital: Social Theory and the Third Way*, Oxford University Press.

Barr, J. (1994) Policy frameworks and policy planning, in *Schooling with Care?*, Scottish Council for Research in Education, Edinburgh.

Barrow, G. (1995) Behaviour support – moving towards an eco-systemic model, *Therapeutic Care and Education*, Vol. 4, no. 2, pp. 48–53.

Barrow, G. (1996) A survey of behaviour support services, *Emotional and Behavioural Difficulties*, Vol. 1, no. 2, pp. 31–34.

Baskind, S. and Thompson, D. (1995) Using assistants to support the educational needs of pupils with learning difficulties, the sublime or the ridiculous, *Educational and Child Psychology*, Vol. 12, no. 2, pp. 46–57.

Bennathan, M. and Boxall, M. (1996) *Effective Interventions in Primary Schools, Nurture Groups*, David Fulton, London.

Bernstein, B. (1977) Aspects of the relations between education and production, in *Class, Codes and Control (Vol. 3)*, Routledge and Kegan Paul, London.

Blatchford, P. and Sumpner, C. (1998) What do we know about breaktime? Results from a national survey of breaktime and lunchtime in primary and secondary schools, *British Educational Journal*, Vol. 24, no. 1, pp. 79–94.

Blyth, E. and Milner, J. (1994) Exclusion from school and victim-blaming, *Oxford Review of Education*, Vol. 20, no. 3, pp. 293–306.

Bond, T. (1986) *Games for Life and Social Skills*, Hutcheson, London.

Bond, T. (1993) *Standards and Ethics for Counselling in Action*, Sage, London.

Booth, T. (1996) Stories of exclusion, natural and unnatural exclusion, in E. Blyth, and J. Milner (eds.) *Exclusion from School; Interprofessional Issues for Policy and Practice*, Routledge, London.

Booth, T. and Ainscow, M. (1998) *From Them to Us. An International Study of Inclusion in Education*, Routledge, London.

Bosker, R. J. and Sheerens, J. (1994) Alternative models of school effectiveness put to the test, in R. J. Bosker, B. P. M. Creemers and J. Scheerens (eds.) *Conceptual and Methodological Advances in Educational Effective Research*, Special issue of *International Journal of Educational Research*,Vol. 2, no. 2, pp. 159–180.

Boulton, M. (1993a) Children's abilities to distinguish between playful and aggressive fighting. A developmental perspective, *British Journal of Developmental Psychology*, Vol. 11, pp. 249–263.

Boulton, M. (1993b) A comparison of adults' and children's abilities to distinguish between aggressive and playful fighting in middle school pupils. Implications for playground supervision and behaviour management, *Educational Studies*, Vol. 19, no. 2, pp. 193–203.

Bourdieu, P. (1986) The forms of capital, reprinted in A. H. Halsey, H. Lauder, P. Brown and A. Stuart Wells (1997) *Education: Culture, Economy, Society*, Oxford University Press.

Bourdieu, P. and Passeron, J. C. (1977) *Reproduction in Education, Society and Culture*, Sage, London.

Bowles, S. and Gintis, H. (1976) *Schooling in Capitalist America*, Routledge and Kegan Paul, London.

Brandes, D. (1982) *Gamesters' Handbook*, Hutcheson, London.

Bridgeland, M. (1971) *Pioneer Work with Maladjusted Children*, Staples, London.

British Association for Counselling (1999) *Code of Ethics and Practice*, BAC, Rugby.

Brodie, I. (1998) *Exclusions from School (Highlight series, No. 161)*, National Children's Bureau, London.

Brodie, I. and Berridge D. (undated) *School Exclusion*, Report on a Research Seminar, University of London.

Bryce, T. and Humes, W. (1999) *Scottish Education*, Edinburgh University Press, Edinburgh.

Bullock, R., Little, M. and Millham, S. (1994) Children's return from state care to school, *Oxford Review of Education*, Vol. 20, no. 3, pp. 307-316.

Canter, L. and Canter, M. (1992) *Assertive Discipline*, Lee Canter Associates, Santa Monica.

Caprara, G. V. and Rutter, M. (1995) Individual development and social change, in M. Rutter and D. Smith (eds.) *Psychosocial Disorders in Young People, Time, Trends and their Causes*, Wiley, London.

Charlton, T. and David, K. (1993) *Managing Misbehaviour in Schools*, 2nd edition, Routledge, London.

Children (Scotland) Act (1995).

Children Act (1989).

Chisholm, S. (1987) Alternative provision for disruptive pupils in rural areas, in

Alternative Approaches to Children with Behavioural Difficulties, SED, Edinburgh.

Clark, C., Dyson, A., Millward, A. and Skidmore, D. (1995) *Towards Inclusive Schools*, David Fulton, London.

Clark, C., Dyson, A., Millward, A., and Robson, S. (1999) Theories of inclusion, theories of schools, deconstructing and reconstructing the 'inclusive school', *British Educational Research Journal*, Vol. 25, no. 2, pp. 157–177.

Clark, M. M. and Munn, P. (1997) *Education in Scotland: Policy and Practice from Pre-school to Secondary*, Routledge, London.

Closs, A. (1996) Katya's kids: Teaching Romany children in Prague, *Multicultural Teaching*, Vol. 14, no. 3, pp. 31–35.

Closs, A. (1997) Special educational provision, in M. M. Clark and P. Munn (eds.) *Education in Scotland, Policy and Practice from Pre-school to Secondary*, Routledge, London.

Cohen, R. and Hughes, M. with Ashworth, L. and Blair, M. (1994) *School's Out, The Family Perspective on School Exclusion*, Barnardo's and Family Service Unit, London.

Cole, T. and Visser, J. (1998) How should the effectiveness of schools for pupils with EBD be assessed? *Emotional and Behavioural Difficulties*, Vol. 3, no. 1, pp. 37–43.

Cole, T., Visser, J. and Upton, G. (1998) *Effective Schooling for Pupils with Emotional and Behavioural Difficulties*, David Fulton, London.

Coleman, J. (1988) Social capital in the creation of human capital, reprinted in A. H. Halsey, H. Lauder, P. Brown and A. Stuart Wells (1997) *Education: Culture, Economy, Society*, Oxford University Press.

Commission for Racial Equality (1996) *Exclusion From School – The Public Cost*, CRE, London.

Cooper, P. (1993) *Effective Schools for Disaffected Students: Integration and Segregation*, Routledge, London.

Cooper, P. (1999a) Changing perceptions of emotional and behavioural difficulties, maladjusted, EBD and beyond, *Emotional and Behavioural Difficulties*, Vol. 4, no. 1, pp. 3–11.

Cooper, P. (1999b) (ed.) *Understanding and Supporting Children with Emotional and Behavioural Difficulties*, Jessica Kingsley, London.

Cooper, P. and Upton, G. (1991) Controlling the urge to control: An ecosystemic approach to problem behaviour in schools, *Support for Learning*, Vol. 6, no. 1, pp. 22–26.

Cooper, P., Smith, C., and Upton, G. (1996) *Emotional and Behavioural Difficulties – Theory to Practice*, Routledge, London.

Cowie, H. and Pecherek, A. (1994) *Counselling, Approaches and Issues in Education*, David Fulton, London.

Cowie, H. and Sharp, S. (1998) *Counselling and Supporting Children in Distress*, Sage, London.

Craig, P. C. (1995) Exploring pupils' perceptions of their experience in secure accommodation, in M. Lloyd-Smith and J. Dwyfor Davies, *On the Margins: The Educational Experiences of 'Problem' Pupils*, Trentham, Stoke.

Cullen, M. A., Fletcher-Campbell, F., Bowen, E., Osgood, J. and Kelleher, S. (forthcoming) *Letting Talents Shine: Guidance on Using Alternative Curriculum Programmes at Key Stage 4*. NFER, Slough.

Cullen, M. A. and Lloyd, G. (1997) *Alternative Educational Provision for Excluded Pupils: A Literature Review*, Moray House, Edinburgh.

Cullen, M. A., Johnstone, M., Lloyd, G. and Munn, P. (1996) *Exclusion from School and Alternatives*, Three Reports to the Scottish Office, Moray House, Edinburgh.

Cullingford, C. and Morrison, J. (1996). Who excludes whom? The personal experience of exclusion, in E. Blyth and J. Milner (eds.) *Exclusion from School: Inter-professional Issues for Policy and Practice*, Routledge, London and New York.

Curry, M. and Bromfield, C. (1994) *Circle Time*, NASEN, Stafford.

de Pear, S. and Garner, P. (1996) Tales from the exclusion zone: The views of teachers and pupils, in E. Blyth and J. Milner (eds.) *Exclusion from School: Inter-professional Issues for Policy and Practice*, Routledge, London and New York.

De Shazer, S. (1991) *Putting Difference to Work*, Norton, New York.

Dearing, R. (1996) *Review of Qualifications for 16–19-Year-Olds: Full report*, SCAA, Hayes.

Department for Education (1994) *The Education of Pupils with Emotional and Behavioural Difficulties*, Circular 9/94, DFE, London.

Department for Education and Employment (1998) *LEA Behaviour Support Plans*, Circular 1/98, DfEE, London.

Department for Education and Employment (1999) *Social Inclusion, Pupil Support*, Circular No 10/99, DfEE, London.

Department of Education and Science (1989) *Discipline in Schools*, The Elton Report, HMSO, London.

Dwivedi, K. N. (1993) *Group Work with Children and Adolescents: A Handbook*, Jessica Kingsley, London.

Dyson, A. (1997) Social and educational disadvantage, reconnecting special needs education, *British Journal of Special Needs Education*, Vol. 14, no. 4, pp. 152–157.

Education (No 2) Act (1986).

Education Act (1997).

Educational Institute for Scotland (1998) *Education and Poverty*, EIS, Edinburgh.

Egan, G. (1994) *The Skilled Helper*, Brooks/Cole, Pacific Grove CA.

Eurydice (1999) Papers provided by the Eurydice Unit for England, Wales and Northern Ireland, NFER, Slough.

Farrell, K. and Tsakalidou, K. (1999) *Recent trends in the re-integration of pupils with emotional and behavioural difficulties in the United Kingdom*, Research report, University of Manchester.

Farrington, D. (1995) The challenge of teenage anti-social behaviour, in M. Rutter (ed.) *Psychosocial Disturbances in Young People*, University of Cambridge.

Federal Register (1999) *Department of Education: Rules and Regulations*, Vol. 64, no. 48, US Government Publication, Washington.

Felsleitner, R. (1999) *Inspectionsbezirk. Sonderpädagogische Zentren für integrative Betreung*, Stadschulrat, Wien.

Ferguson, R., Lloyd, G. and Reid, G. (1997) *Attention Deficit and Hyperactivity Disorder: A Literature Review*, Moray House Publications, Edinburgh.

Fielding, M. (1999) Communities of learners, in B. O'Hagan (ed.) *Modern Educational Myths*, Kogan Page, London.

Fletcher Campbell, F. and Hall, C. (1991) *Changing Schools, Changing People*, NFER Nelson, Slough.

G.B. Statutes (1998) *The Education (National Curriculum) (Exceptions at Key Stage 4) Regulations 1998*, Statutory Instruments, no. 2021, Education, England and Wales, The Stationery Office, London.

Gable, R. A., Sugai, G., Lewis, T., Nelson, J. R., Cheney, D., Safran, S. P. and Safran, J. S. (1998) *Individual and Systemic Approaches to Collaboration and Consultation on Behalf of Students with Emotional/Behavioural Disorders*, Council for Children with Behavioural Disorders, Reston, VA.

Galloway, D., Armstrong, D. and Tomlinson, S. (1994) *The Assessment of Special Educational Needs: Whose Problem*, Longman, London.

Gamarnikov, E. and Green, A. (1999) Developing social capital, dilemmas, possibilities and limitations in education, in A. Hayton (ed.) *Tackling Disaffection and Social Exclusion*, Kogan Page, London.

Gamoran, A., Nystrand, M., Berends, M. and Lepore, P. C. (1995) An organisational analysis of the effects of ability grouping, *American Educational Research Journal*, Vol. 32, no. 5, pp. 687–715.

Garner, P. (1992) Involving 'disruptive' students in school discipline structures, *Pastoral Care in Education*, Vol. 10, no. 3, pp. 13–19.

Garner, P. (1995) Schools by scoundrels, the views of 'disruptive' pupils in mainstream schools in England and the USA, in M. Lloyd Smith and J. Dwyfor Davies, *On the Margins. The Educational Experience of 'Problem' Pupils*, Trentham, Stoke.

Geldard, K. and Geldard, D. (1997) *Counselling Children*, Sage, London.

Geldard, K. and Geldard, D. (1999) *Counselling Adolescents: The Proactive Approach*, Sage, London.

Gilborn, D. (1998) Exclusion from school, an overview of the issues, in New Policy Institute (ed.) *Second Chances, Exclusion from School and Equality of Opportunity*, New Policy Institute, London.

Glennerster, H. (1998) Tackling poverty at its roots? Education, in C. Oppenheim (ed.) *An Inclusive Society, Strategies for Tackling Poverty*, Institute for Public Policy Research, London.

Goleman, D. (1996) *Emotional Intelligence*, Bloomsbury, London.

Gray, P. and Noakes, J. (1993) Reintegration of children with challenging behaviours into the mainstream school community, in A. Miller and D. Lane (eds.) *Silent Conspiracies, Scandals and Success in the Care and Education of Vulnerable Young People*, Trentham, Stoke.

Gray, P., Miller, A. and Noakes, J. (eds.) (1994) *Challenging Behaviour in Schools*, Routledge, London.

Grimshaw, R. and Berridge D (1994) *Educating Disruptive Children, Placement and Process in Residential Special Schools for Pupils with Emotional and Behavioural Difficulties*, National Children's Bureau, London.

Hallett, C. and Hazel, N. (1998) *The Evaluation of Children's Hearings in Scotland. The International Context: Trends in Juvenile Justice and Child Welfare*, Scottish Office Research Unit, Edinburgh.

Hallett, C. and Murray, C. with Jamieson, H. and Veitch, B. (1998) *The Evaluation of Children's Hearings in Scotland. Deciding in Children's Interests*, The Scottish Office, Edinburgh.

Halsey, A. (1972) *Educational Priority, EPA Problems and Policies*, Vol. 1, HMSO, London.

Halsey, A. H., Lauder, H., Brown, P. and Wells, A. S. (1997) *Education: Culture, Economy, Society*, Oxford University Press.

Hargreaves, A. (1980) Synthesis and the study of strategies: a project for the sociological imagination, in P. Woods (ed.) *Pupil Strategies: Explorations in the Sociology of the Secondary School*, Croom Helm, London.

Hargreaves, D. H., Hester, J. K. and Mellor, F. J. (1975) *Deviance in Classrooms*, Routledge and Kegan Paul, London.

Hayden, C. (1997) *Children Excluded from School, Debates, Evidence, Responses*, Open University Press, Buckingham and Philadelphia.

Hill, M., Trisiliotis, J. and Borland, M. (1995) Social work services for young people, in M. Hill, R. Hawthorne Kirk, and D. Part (eds.) *Supporting Families*, HMSO, Edinburgh.

HMI (1990) *Choosing with Care: A Report on the Provision for Pupils with Behavioural, Emotional and Social Difficulties*, Scottish Office Education Department, Edinburgh.

HMI (1996) *Standards and Quality in Scottish Schools 1992–95*, Scottish Office, Edinburgh.

HMSO (1991) *Children in the Public Care: A Review of Residential Care*, The Utting Report, HMSO, London.

Hodgson, A. and Spours, K. (1999) *New Labour's Educational Agenda, Issues and Policies for Education and Training from 14+*, London, Kogan Page.

Holland, P. and Homerton, P. (1994) Balancing school and individual approaches, in P. Gray, A. Miller, and J. Noakes (eds.) *Challenging Behaviour in Schools: Teacher Support, Practical Techniques and Policy Development*, Routledge, London.

Hopmann, S. and Konzuli, R. (1997) Close our schools! Against trends in policy-making, educational theory and curriculum studies, *Journal of Curriculum Studies*, Vol. 29, no. 3, pp. 259–266.

Imich, A. (1994) Exclusions from school, current trends and issues, *Educational Research*, Vol. 36, no. 1, pp. 3–11.

Jackson, S. (1987) *The Education of Children in Care*, University of Bristol.

John, P. (1996) Damaged Goods? An interpretation of excluded pupils' perceptions of schooling, in E. Blyth and J. Milner (eds.) *Exclusion from School: Inter-professional Issues for Policy and Practice*, Routledge, London and New York.

John, P. D. and Osborn, A. (1992) The influence of school ethos on pupils' citizenship attitudes, *Educational Review*, Vol. 44, no. 2, pp. 153–165.

Johnstone, M. and Munn, P. (1997) *Primary and Secondary Teachers' Perceptions of Indiscipline*, Confidential Report to the Educational Institute of Scotland, Moray House Publications, Edinburgh.

Jones, N. and Jones, E. (eds.) (1992) *Learning to Behave*, Kogan Page, London.

Kahan, B. (1994) *Growing Up In Groups*, HMSO, London.

Kendrick, A. (1995) The integration of child care services in Scotland, *Children and Youth Services Review*, Vol. 17, no. 5/6, pp. 619–635.

Kinder, K. and Wilkin, A. (1998) *With All Respect, Reviewing Disaffection Strategies*, NFER, Slough.

Kinder, K., Harland, J., Wilkin, A. and Wakefield, A. (1995) *Three to Remember, Strategies for Disaffected Pupils*, NFER, Slough.

Kinder, K., Kendall, S., Downing, D., Atkinson, M. and Hogarth, S. (1999a) *Nil Exclusion? Policy and Practice*, Slough, NFER.

Kinder, K., Kendall, S., Halsey, K., Atkinson, M. (1999b) *Disaffection Talks. A Report for the Merseyside Learning Partnership Inter Agency Development Programme*, NFER, Slough.

Kinder, K., Wilkin, A., Wakefield, D. A. (1997) *Exclusion: Who Needs It?* NFER, Slough.

Knapp, M. and Fenyo, A. (1994) *The Cost and Cost Effectiveness of Intermediate Treatment*, Report to the Department of Health, Personal Social Services Department, University of Kent.

Lane, D. (1994) Supporting effective responses to challenging behaviour: from theory to practice, in P. Gray, A. Miller and J. Noakes (eds.) *Challenging Behaviour in Schools*, Routledge, London.

Lang, P. (1999) Counselling, counselling skills and encouraging pupils to talk: Clarifying and addressing confusion, *British Journal of Guidance and Counselling*, Vol. 27, no. 1, pp. 23–33.

Langford, P., Lovegrove, H. and Lovegrove, M. (1994) Do senior secondary school students possess the moral maturity to negotiate class rules? *Journal of Moral Education*, Vol. 23, no. 4, pp. 387–407.

Lawrence, B. and Hayden, C. (1997) Primary school exclusions, *Educational Research and Evaluation*, Vol. 3, no. 1, pp. 54–77.

Layzell, P. (1995) A case study of a parental involvement scheme, *Therapeutic Care and Education*, Vol. 4, no. 2, pp. 30–35.

Lee, B. and Mawson, C. (1998) *Survey of Classroom Assistants*, NFER, Slough.

Leney, T. (1999) European approaches to social exclusion, in A. Hayton (ed.) *Tackling Disaffection and Social Exclusion*, Kogan Page, London.

Levin, H. M. and Kelley, C. (1994) Can education do it alone?, reprinted in A. H. Halsey, H. Lauder, P. Brown and A. Stuart Wells (1997) *Education: Culture, Economy, Society*, Oxford University Press.

Lipsky, D. K. and Gartner, A. (1997) *Inclusion and School Reform, Transforming America's Classrooms*, Paul H. Brookes, Baltimore.

Littlewood, P. (1996) Secure units, in S. Asquith, *Children and Young People in Conflict with the Law*, Jessica Kingsley, London.

Lloyd, G. (ed.) (1992) *Chosen with Care? Responding to Disruptive and Disturbing Behaviour*, Moray House Publications, Edinburgh.

Lloyd, G. (1997) Can the law support children's rights in schools in Scotland and prevent the development of a climate of blame? *Pastoral Care in Education*, September, pp. 13–16.

Lloyd, G. (1999a) Ethical and supervision issues in the use of counselling and other helping skills with children and young people in school, *Pastoral Care*, Vol. 17, no. 3, pp. 25–30.

Lloyd, G. (1999b) Gender and exclusion from school, in J. Salisbury and S. Riddell, *Gender, Policy and Educational Change*, Routledge, London.

Lloyd, G. and Norris, C. (1999) Including ADHD?, *Disability and Society*, Vol. 14.

Lloyd, G. and O'Regan A. (1999) Education for social exclusion? Issues to do with the effectiveness of educational provision for young women with 'social, emotional and behavioural difficulties', *Emotional and Behavioural Difficulties*, Vol. 4, no. 2, pp. 38–46.

Lloyd, G. and Padfield, P. (1996) Reintegration into mainstream. 'Gi'e us peace!' *British Journal Of Special Education*, Vol. 23, no. 4, pp. 180–186.

Lloyd, G., Stead, J., Jordan, E. and Norris, C. (1999) Teachers and Gypsy Travellers, *Scottish Educational Review*, Vol. 31, no. 1, pp. 48–65.

Lloyd-Smith, M. (1993) *Problem behaviour, Exclusions and the Policy Vacuum*, Pastoral care: Vol 11, no. 4, pp. 19–24.

Lloyd-Smith, M. and Dwyfor Davies, J. (eds.) (1995) *On the Margins: The Educational Experiences of 'Problem' Pupils*, Trentham, Stoke.

Lothian Regional Council (1989) Report of the Working Group on Secondary Age Children with Social Emotional and Behavioural Difficulties, Edinburgh.

MacDonald, B. (1989) *Murder in the Playground* (Burnage Enquiry), Longsight Press, London.

MacIvor, I. and Martin, R. (1987) Alternative approaches to pupils with behavioural/emotional problems, in SED, *Alternative Approaches to Children with Behavioural Difficulties*, SED, Edinburgh.

MacPhee, H. (1992) Assessment – what is the problem? in G. Lloyd (ed.) *Chosen with Care? Responses to Disturbing and Disruptive Behaviour*, Moray House Publications, Edinburgh.

Maines, B. and Robinson, G. (1995) Assertive discipline – no wheels on your wagon – a reply to Swinson and Melling, *Educational Psychology in Practice*, Vol. 11, no. 3, pp. 9-11.

Mallon, B. (1998) *Helping Children Manage Loss, Positive Strategies for Renewal and Growth*, Jessica Kingsley, London.

Maxwell, W. S. (1995) *Effective Provision for Pupils with Social, Emotional and Behavioural Difficulties*, Conference Paper, Scottish Support for Learning Association, 13 May, Orkney.

MBI (1999) *Montana Behavioural Initiative Information Leaflet*, State of Montana.

McGuire, J. (1997) Psycho-social approaches to the understanding and reduction of violence in young people, in V. Varma, *Violence in Children and Adolescents,* Jessica Kingsley, London.

McKay, B. (1994) Inter-agency approaches, in P. Munn (ed.) *Schooling with Care,* Scottish Council for Research in Education, Edinburgh.

McLaughlin, C. (1999) Counselling in schools: looking back and looking forward, *British Journal of Guidance and Counselling*, Vol. 27, no. 1, pp. 13–22.

McLean, A. and Brown, J. (1992) Developing a school support service for children with social, emotional and behavioural difficulties, in G. Lloyd (ed.) *Chosen with Care? Responding to Disruptive and Disturbing Behaviour*, Moray House Publications, Edinburgh.

McNeill, B. (1996) Behaviour support in a mainstream school, *Support for Learning*, Vol. 11, no. 4, pp. 181-184.

McPherson, A. and Raab, C. (1998) *Governing Education*, Edinburgh University Press.

Mellor, A. (1999) Victims of bullying, in H. Kemshall and J. Prichard (eds.) *Good Practice in Working with Victims of Violence*, Jessica Kingsley, London.

Merrett, F. and Merrett, F. (1992) Classroom management for project work: an application of correspondence training, *Educational Studies*, Vol. 18, no. 1, pp. 3–10.

Miller, A. (1994) Mainstream teachers talking about successful behaviour support, in P. Gray, A. Miller and J. Noakes (eds.) *Challenging Behaviour in Schools*, Routledge, London.

Mills, C. W. (1959) *The Sociological Imagination*, Penguin, Harmondsworth.

Mitchell, L. (1996) The effects of waiting time on excluded children, in E. Blyth and J. Milner (eds.) *Exclusion from School; Inter-Professional Issues for Policy and Practice*, Routledge, London.

Mortimore, P. and Whitty, G. (1999) School improvement: a remedy for social exclusion? in A. Hayton (ed.) *Tackling Disaffection and Social Exclusion*, Kogan Page, London.

Mortimore, P., Sammons, P., Stoll, L., Lewis, D. and Ecob, R. (1988) *School Matters, The Junior Years*, Paul Chapman, London.

Mosley, J. (1999) *More Quality Circle Time*, LDA, Wisbech.

Munn, P. (1994) The role of the learning support teacher in Scottish primary and secondary classrooms, in S. Riddell and S. Brown, *Special Educational Needs Policy in the 1990s. Warnock in the Market Place*, Routledge, London.

Munn, P. (1997) Devolved management of schools, in M. M. Clark and P. Munn (eds.) *Education in Scotland, Policy and Practice from Pre-school to Secondary*, Routledge, London.

Munn, P. (1999a) The darker side of pupil culture, in J. Prosser (ed.) *School Culture*, Paul Chapman, London.

Munn, P. (ed.) (1999b) *Promoting Positive Discipline in Scottish Schools, Whole School Approaches to Tackling Low Level Disruption*, Faculty of Education, Edinburgh.

Munn, P. and Lloyd, G. (forthcoming) *Indiscipline in Schools: A Review of Extent, 'Causes' and 'Cures'*, Scottish Council for Research in Education, Edinburgh.

Munn, P., Johnstone, M. and Chalmers, V. (1992a) *Effective Discipline in Secondary Schools and Classrooms*, Paul Chapman, London.

Munn, P., Johnstone, M. and Chalmers, V. (1992b) *Effective Discipline in Primary Schools and Classrooms*, Paul Chapman, London.

Munn, P., Johnstone, M. and Sharp, S. (1998) Is indiscipline getting worse? Scottish teachers' perceptions of indiscipline in 1990 and 1996, *Scottish Educational Review*, Vol. 30, no. 2, pp. 157–172.

Munn, P., Cullen, M. A., Johnstone, M. and Lloyd, G. (1997) *Exclusion from School* and In-School Alternatives, Interchange 47, Scottish Office, Edinburgh.

Munn, P., Cullen, M. A., Johnstone, M. and Lloyd, G. (2000) Exclusion from school. A view from Scotland of some policy and practice dilemmas, *Scottish Affairs*, no. 2.

National Commission on Education (1996) *Success Against The Odds: Effective Schools in Disadvantaged Areas*, Routledge, London.

Newsom (1963) *Half our Future*, Report for the Ministry of Education, London, HMSO.

Normington, J. (1992) Return to school from an assessment centre, in G. Vulliamy and R. Webb (eds.) *Teacher Research and Special Educational Needs*, David Fulton, London.

Normington, J. and Kyriacou, C. (1994) Exclusion from high schools and the work of the outside agencies involved, *Pastoral Care in Education*, Vol. 12, no. 4, pp. 12–15.

Norwich, B. (1997) *A Trend Towards Inclusion, Statistics on Special School Placements and Pupils with Statements in Ordinary Schools, England 1992–96*, Centre for Studies on Inclusive Education, London.

O'Rourke, K. and Worzbyt, J. (1996) *Support Groups for Children*, Taylor and Francis, London.

Ofsted (1993) *Education for Disaffected Pupils 1990–92*, DfE, London.

Ofsted (1995) *Pupil Referral Units: The First Twelve Inspections*, A Report from the Office of Her Majesty's Chief Inspector of Schools, DfE, London.

Ofsted (1996) *The Education of Travelling Pupils*, DfE, London.

Osler, A. and Hill, J. (1999) Exclusion from school and racial equality: an examination of government proposals in the light of recent research evidence, *Cambridge Journal of Education*, Vol. 29, no. 1, pp. 33–62.

Parsons, C. (1996a) Permanent exclusions from school in England, trends, causes and responses, *Children and Society*, Vol. 10, pp. 177–186.

Parsons, C. (1996b) The cost of primary school exclusions, in E. Blyth and J. Milner (eds.) *Exclusion from School: Inter-professional Issues for Policy and Practice*, Routledge, London.

Parsons, C. (1999) *Education, Exclusion and Citizenship*, Routledge, London.

Parsons, C., Benns, L., Hailes, J. and Howlett, K. (1994) *Excluding Primary School Children*, Family Policy Studies Centre and Joseph Rowntree, London.

Parsons, C., Hailes, J., Howlett, K., Davies, A., Driscoll, P. and Ross, L. (1995) *National Survey of Local Education Authorities' Policies and Procedures for the Identification of, and Provision for, Children Who are Out of School by Reasons of Exclusion or Otherwise*, DfEE, London.

Paterson, L. (1997) Policy making in Scottish education: a case of pragmatic nationalism, in M. M. Clark and P. Munn (eds.) *Education in Scotland, Policy and Practice from Pre-school to Secondary*, Routledge, London.

Pellegrini, A. D. and Smith, P. K. (1993) School recess, implications for education and development, *Review of Educational Research*, Vol. 63, pp. 51–67.

Petrie, M. and Shaw, M. (1998) The disability movement and the struggle for inclusion, in J. Crowther, I. Martin and M. Shaw (eds.) *Popular Education and Social Movements in Scotland Today*, National Institute for Adult and Continuing Education, Leicester.

Pijl, S. J. and Meijer, C. J. W. (1991) Does integration count for much? An analysis of the process of integration in eight countries, *European Journal of Special Needs Education*, Vol. 3, no. 2, pp. 63–73.

Portes, A. (1998) Social capital: its origins and applications in modern sociology, *Annual Review of Sociology*, Vol. 24, pp. 1–24.

Poverty Alliance (1998) *Social Inclusion in Scotland. A Framework for Development*,

A response to the Scottish Office Consultation Paper 'Social Exclusion in Scotland', Poverty Alliance, Glasgow.

Priestley, P. H. (1987) The future of residential schools for the maladjusted, *Maladjustment and Therapeutic Education*, Vol. 5, no. 2, pp. 30–37.

Pritchard, B. and Barker, K. (1996) Negotiating a classroom contract, *Modern English Teacher*, Vol. 5, no. 1, pp. 45–47.

Qualifications and Curriculum Authority (1998) *Disapplication of the National Curriculum at Key Stage 4: Guidance for Schools*, QCA, London.

Quayle, W. and Holdsworth, J. (1997) Self esteem groups at the Eleanor Smith School and primary support service, *Emotional and Behavioural Difficulties*, Vol. 2, no. 2, pp. 21–24.

Quick, E. K. (1996) *Doing What Works in Brief Therapy. A Strategic Solution Focused Approach*, Academic Press, London.

Raffe, D. (1997) Upper secondary education, in M. M. Clark and P. Munn (eds.) *Education in Scotland, Policy and Practice from Pre-school to Secondary*, Routledge, London.

Rathbone CI (1999) *Behaviour Support Plans*, Rathbone CI, Manchester.

Reezigt, G. J. and Pijl, S. J. (1998) The Netherlands: a springboard for other initiatives, in T. Booth and M. Ainscow, *From Them to Us. An International Study of Inclusion in Education*, Routledge, London.

Rennie, E. (1993) Behavioural support teaching, points to ponder, *Support for Learning*, Vol. 8, no. 1, pp. 7–10.

Reynolds, D. (1997) School effectiveness, retrospect and prospect, *Scottish Educational Review*, Vol. 29, no. 2, pp. 97–113.

Rhodes, J. and Ajmal, Y. (1995) *Solution Focussed Thinking in Schools, Behaviour, Reading and Organisation*, BT, London.

Riddell, S. and Brown, S. (eds.) (1994) *Special Educational Policy in the 1990s. Warnock in the Marketplace*, Routledge, London.

Robinson, G. and Maines, B. (1994a) Assertive discipline – jumping on a dated bandwagon, *Educational Psychology in Practice*, Vol. 9, no. 4, pp. 195–200.

Robinson, G. and Maines, B. (1994b) Who manages pupil behaviour? Assertive discipline – a blunt instrument for a fine task, *Pastoral Care in Education*, Vol. 12, no. 3, pp. 30–35.

Rodger, D. (1994) *An Evaluation of the Possilpark Befriending Project*, Argyll Publishing, Glendaruel.

Ruddock, J., Chaplain, R. and Wallace, G. (1996) *School Improvement, What Can Pupils Tell Us?*, David Fulton, London.

Russell, R. (1997) Classroom management strategies in a primary school class, in G. Lloyd and P. Munn (eds.) *Sharing Good Practice*, Moray House Publications, Edinburgh.

Rutter, M. and Smith, D. (1995) *Psychosocial Disorders in Young People, Time, Trends and their Causes*, Wiley, London.

Rutter, M., Maungham, B., Mortimore, P. and Ouston, J. (1979) *Fifteen Thousand Hours, Secondary Schools and Their Effects on Children*, Paul Chapman, London.

Sammons, P., Thomas, S. and Mortimore, P. (1997) *Forging Links, Effective Schools and Effective Departments*, Paul Chapman, London.

Sandow, S. (1994) More ways than one, models of special needs, in S. Sandow (ed.) *Whose Special Need?*, Paul Chapman, London.

School Standards and Framework Act (1998).

Scottish Office (1964) *Report on Children and Young Persons* (The Kilbrandan Report), HMSO, Edinburgh.

Scottish Office (1998) *Guidance on Issues Concerning Exclusion from School*, Circular No 2/98, Scottish Office, Edinburgh.

168   *Alternatives to Exclusion from School*

Scottish Office (1999) *New Community Schools Prospectus*, Scottish Office, Edinburgh.
Scottish Office (undated) *Social Inclusion, Opening the Door to a Better Scotland*, Scottish Office, Edinburgh.
SED (1977) *Truancy and Indiscipline in Scottish Schools* (The Pack Report), HMSO, Edinburgh.
SEED (1999) *Research Specification, Curriculum Provision for Disaffected Young People*, Edinburgh, SEED.
Sharp, P. (1997) Primary–secondary transition programme: a better chance of success, in G. Lloyd and P. Munn (eds.) *Sharing Good Practice*, Moray House Publications, Edinburgh.
Sharp, S. and Cowie, H. (1998) *Counselling and Supporting Children in Distress*, Sage, London.
Simpson, D. (1992) Panmure House School groups: one approach to dealing with young people's schooling difficulties, in G. Lloyd, (ed.) *Chosen with Care? Responding to Disruptive and Disturbing Behaviour*, Moray House Publications, Edinburgh.
Sinclair Taylor, A. (1995) A dunce's place, pupils' perceptions of the role of a special unit, in M. Lloyd Smith and J. Dwyfor Davies, *On the Margins. The Educational Experience of 'Problem' Pupils*, Trentham, Stoke.
Sinclair, G. (1999) Positive approaches to behaviour in Banff Academy, in P. Munn (ed.) *Promoting Positive Discipline in Scottish Schools: Whole School Approaches to Tackling Low Level Disruption*, Faculty of Education, Edinburgh.
Slee, R. (1995) *Changing Theories and Practices of Discipline*, Falmer, London.
Smith, D. (1995) *Towards Explaining Patterns and Trends in Youth Crime in Psychosocial Disturbances in Young People*, Cambridge University Press.
Smith, I. (1998) *Is Praise Always a Good Thing?* Scottish Consultative Council on the Curriculum, Dundee.
Smith, P., Morita, Y., Junger-Tas, J., Olweus, D., Catalanot, E. and Slee, P. (1999) (eds.) *The Nature of School Bullying – A Cross Cultural Perspective*, Routledge, London.
Smout, T. C. (1969) *A History of the Scottish People 1560–1830*, Fontana, Glasgow.
Social Exclusion Unit (1998) *Truancy and Social Exclusion*, The Stationery Office, London.
SOED (1992a) *Using Ethos Indicators in Primary School Self-Evaluation*, HM Inspectors of Schools, Edinburgh.
SOED (1992b) *Using Ethos Indicators in Secondary School Self-Evaluation*, HM Inspectors of Schools, Edinburgh.
SOEID (1996) *How Good is Our School?* Scottish Office, Edinburgh.
SSI/Ofsted (Social Services Inspectorate/Office for Standards in Education) (1995) *The Education of Children who are Looked After by Local Authorities*, Department of Health/Ofsted, London.
Stacey, H. (1996) Mediation into schools does go. An outline of the mediation process, *Pastoral Care in Education*, Vol. 14, no. 2, pp. 7–9.
Stirling, M. (1992) How many pupils are being excluded? *British Journal of Special Education*, Vol. 19, no. 4, pp. 128–130.
Stirling, M. (1993) A black mark against him? Why are African-Caribbean boys over represented in the excluded pupil population? *Multicultural Education Review*, Vol. 15, pp. 3–6.
Stirling, M. (1994) The end of the line, *Special Children*, Vol. 76, pp. 27–29.
Sukhnandan, L. with Lee, B. (1998) *Streaming, Setting and Grouping by Ability: A Review of the Literature*, NFER, Slough.
Swinson, J. and Melling, R. (1995) Assertive discipline – four wheels on this wagon

– a reply to Robinson and Maines, *Educational Psychology in Practice*, Vol. 11, no. 3, pp. 3-8.

Thomson, G., Stewart, M. and Ward, K. (1996) *Criteria for Opening Records of Needs*, Interchange 40, Scottish Office, Edinburgh.

Tisdall, K. (1996) From the Social Work (Scotland) Act 1968 to the Children Act (Scotland) 1995. Pressure for change, in M. Hill and J. Aldgate (eds.) *Child Welfare Services*, Jessica Kingsley, London.

Tizard, B., Blatchford, P., Burke, J., Farquhar, C. and Plewis, I. (1988) *Young Children at School in the Inner City*, Lawrence Erlbaum Associates, Hove.

Topping, K. (1983) *Educational Systems for Disruptive Adolescents*, Croom Helm, London.

Traxson, D. (1994) Helping children to become more self-directing in their behaviour, in P. Gray, A. Miller and J. Noakes (eds.) *Challenging Behaviour in Schools*, Routledge, London.

Tutt, N. (1984) *Assessment of young people – intentions and outcomes*. Report of a day conference held in Edinburgh, Scottish Intermediate Treatment Resource Centre and Moray House College of Education, Edinburgh.

Upton, G. and Cooper, P. (1990) A new perspective on behaviour problems in schools, the ecosystemic approach, *Maladjustment and Therapeutic Education*, Vol. 8, no. 1, pp. 3–18.

US Department of Education (1998a) *Early Warning Timely Response. A Guide to Safer Schools*, Department for Education, Washington.

US Department of Education (1998b) *To Assure the Free Appropriate Public Education of all Children with Disabilities*, Twentieth Annual Report to Congress on the Implementation of the Individuals with Disabilities Education Act, Department for Education, Washington.

Vulliamy, G. and Webb, R. (1992) (eds.) *Teacher Research and Special Educational Needs*, London, David Fulton.

Walgrave, L. (1996) Restorative juvenile justice: a way to restore justice in Western European systems, in S. Asquith, *Children and Young People in Conflict with the Law*, Jessica Kingsley, London.

Walker, H. M., Steiber, S. and O'Neil, R. E. (1990) Middle school behavioural profiles of anti-social and at-risk boys: descriptive and prescriptive outcomes, *Exceptionally*, Vol. 1, no. 1, pp. 61–78.

Ward, J. (1993) Special education in Australia and New Zealand, in P. Mittler, P. Brouillette and D. Harris, *World Yearbook of Education: Special Educational Needs*, Kogan Page, London.

Warden, D. and Christie, D. (1997) *Teaching Social Behaviour*, David Fulton, London.

Ware, L. (1998) USA: I kind of wonder if we're fooling ourselves, in T. Booth and M. Ainscow, *From Them to Us*, Routledge, London.

Webster's (1986) *Third New International Dictionary*, Encyclopedia Britannica, London.

Weiner, G., Arnot, M. and David, M. (1997) Is the future female? Female success, male disadvantage and changing gender patterns in education, in A. H. Halsey, H. Lauder, P. Brown and A. S. Wells (eds.) *Education: Culture, Economy, Society*, Oxford University Press.

Wheelock, A. (1999) *Safe to be Smart, Building a Culture for Standards-Based Reform in the Middle Grades*, National Middle Schools Association, Ohio.

White, J. and Barber, M. (eds.) (1997) *Perspectives on School Effectiveness and School Improvement*, Institute of Education, London.

Wilson, P. (1996) *Mental Health in Your School*, Jessica Kingsley, London.

Young Minds (1999) *Response to Government Draft Guidance on Social Inclusion: Pupil Support*, Young Minds, London.

Appendix 1: Education in Scotland: Key Facts and Figures

The information in this appendix is largely summarised from Clark and Munn (1997) *Education in Scotland*, published by Routledge. More detailed information can be found there and in Bryce and Humes (1999) *Scottish Education*, published by Edinburgh University Press. Information on Scottish education statistics and policy can be found on the Scottish Executive website at http://www.scotland.gov.uk/

1 Scotland

- Scotland has a population of about five million and is part of the United Kingdom (which includes England, Wales and Northern Ireland) with a total population of around 58 million. It is the most sparsely populated part of the United Kingdom.
- There are high levels of poverty in some areas. For example in 1995 about 20 per cent of the school population were entitled to free school meals; this varied from about 6 per cent in Borders Region to around 40 per cent in Glasgow.
- According to the 1991 census, 98.7 per cent of the population in Scotland were white. Thus only 1.3 per cent of the population were from ethnic minorities of whom the vast majority were of Pakistani or Indian origin.

2 Governance

- Education is a devolved responsibility to the Scottish Parliament. An Education Minister, who is a member of the Scottish Executive, is supported by two junior Ministerial colleagues. There is also a Parliamentary Select Committee.
- The national administration of school education is carried out by civil servants in the Scottish Education Department, now Scottish Executive Education Department, in Edinburgh. There has been a

170

separate education civil service in Scotland for well over a hundred years.

- Numbers of Her Majesty's Inspectors fluctuate around 100. They are led and managed by a senior chief inspector who is also the principal professional adviser to the Scottish Executive. HMI carry out inspections on the performance of schools, teacher education institutions and education authorities. They also frequently take the lead in major curriculum and other policy development. (Ofsted does not operate in Scotland.)
- There are 32 single tier local authorities. These were established in 1996 and replaced a system of nine Regional and three Island Authorities, having responsibility for education. All authorities have an Education Committee, with the majority of members being councillors. All also have a Director of Education who leads and manages education officials, curriculum advisers and development officers.
- The policy emphasis is on school improvement through school self-evaluation, with schools being provided with a set of national and local guides to help them assess their achievements and plan for improvements.
- The General Teaching Council, in existence since 1966, regulates entry to the teaching profession and mainstream professional standards. All teachers in state primary and secondary school are required to be registered with the Teaching Council.

3 Schools

- Most schools are comprehensive and take boys and girls.
- Catholic schools are part of the state sector.
- There is a small number of independent schools run without any aid from public funds. Less than 6 per cent of the pupil population attends these schools.
- There are about 400 secondary schools and 2,300 primary schools and 200 special schools. The independent sector has over 100 schools, many of which are in Edinburgh and Glasgow. Table A1.1 provides details drawn from the Scottish Executive website.
- There are no sixth form colleges. The two formerly grant maintained schools were re-absorbed into local authorities by the Education Act 2000.
- Children spend seven years in primary school, entering around the age of five and leaving around the age of twelve. They spend a minimum of four years at secondary school, the statutory leaving age being 16, although increasing numbers stay on for either one or two further years.
- Pre-school provision includes state, voluntary sector and private nurseries and playgroups.

Table A1.1. Numbers of Scottish schools and teachers

	Schools	Pupil numbers
Secondary	403	315,789
Primary	2,313	441,691
Pre-school (EA)	1,200	
Pre-school (private/voluntary)	1,100	60,000
Independent primary	73	11,197
Independent secondary	57	14,955

4 Curriculum and assessment

- There is no national curriculum as in England and Wales.
- There is a curriculum programme for 5–14-year-olds constructed in terms of five broad areas, and designed to promote breadth, balance and continuity in children's learning. Each area has a guideline advising on curriculum and assessment. The five areas are Language, Mathematics, Expressive Arts, Environmental Studies and Religious and Moral Education. National testing takes place only in English and mathematics with pupils taking tests when teachers believe they are ready to do so. The tests are used as confirmation of teacher judgements and results remain confidential to the school, pupil and parents. There are no performance tables of primary schools based on national test results.
- The five areas of the curriculum in primary school transform themselves into eight 'modes' which structure the curriculum in secondary school. A common course is followed by pupils in the first two years of secondary. Years three and four culminate in Standard Grade examinations with most pupils taking seven or eight, which include one subject from each mode. There are three main grades of assessment, Credit, General and Foundation.
- The upper secondary curriculum has recently been reformed to introduce a unified system of curriculum and assessment to cover all academic and vocational education beyond S4 and below the level of higher education. The benchmark qualification remains the Higher but there will be levels above this, Advanced Higher, and staging posts towards Higher, Intermediate Levels 1 and 2. There are also Scottish Group Awards planned, some of which will be broadly based while others will be more specialised.
- There is one national examinations body, the Scottish Qualifications Authority, following the merger of the Scottish Examination Board and the Scottish Vocational Education Council in 1997.

Appendix 2: The Scottish Children's Hearing System

The welfare orientation of the Children's Hearing System is an important influence on the culture of work with children and young people in difficulty in Scotland. The Hearing System began operating in 1971, following legislation in 1968 based on the Kilbrandon Report, which argued strongly for a social education principle rather than a punitive approach to children in difficulty (Scottish Office, 1964). The system provides a structure of intervention and support for children who are considered to require compulsory measures of care and/or control. Decisions are made on the basis of a comprehensive assessment of the child's needs and in his/her best interests. The Hearings offer a formal process in an informal setting, where parents and children can understand the proceedings and the information on which decisions are made.

There is a broad range of criteria for referral including being beyond the control of parents, not being adequately cared for, exposure to moral danger, abuse, non-attendance at school, solvent abuse, and offending (the full list is given below). The legislation was deliberate in placing offending last on the list of grounds of referral, to emphasise that the Hearing system was for children in difficulty, including, but not exclusively, those who commit crimes. The largest number of referrals does involve offending but many of these will be diverted and never involve attending a Hearing. In recent years referrals for child abuse have increased most rapidly, in parallel with the greater recognition of, and response to, abuse in other Western countries.

The Reporter, often a qualified solicitor, is the gatekeeper to the system, receiving referrals and initially assessing their sufficiency of evidence and the likelihood that the child may be in need of compulsory measures of intervention. In many cases the Reporter may decide that the family is coping well and does not require support, or that they would be willing to accept support informally. There is a broad consensus that formal intervention should be a last resort. Decisions about intervention are made at Hearings by lay people, trained part-time volunteers from the community, called Panel Members. It was intended that the Panel should represent the community in its composition. A recent substantial research project, funded by the Scottish Office, found that this 'has remained an important (although as yet not yet fully achieved) aspiration' (Hallett *et al.*, 1998). Hearings may impose supervision orders, at home or in a residential setting, but may also require a range of other actions. The Children Act (Scotland) 1995 widened the scope of the Hearings by referring to the wider role of councils in children's care and welfare beyond that of the social work department. Thus a requirement of action may be placed also on an educational establishment.

The research report mentioned earlier concluded that:

> Overall there was widespread support for the Children's Hearing System and the principle on which it was based, despite some evidence of tensions and difficulties in practice. These included concerns about its capacity to meet the needs of some children and young people referred (particularly young people who continue to offend and those referred on the grounds of non-attendance at school), widespread frustration about the shortage of resources and an acknowledgement that the emphasis on participation, informality and the provision of help in a welfare framework may be less apparent to some children, young people and parents appearing at the hearing than it is to others.
>
> (Hallett *et al.*, 1998)

Grounds for referral of children to Reporter and to Children's Hearing

Occasions for referring a child to the Reporter

A child may be in need of compulsory measures of supervision if any of the following conditions is satisfied with respect to him *(sic)* (Section 52(2) of The Children (Scotland) Act 1995).

- is beyond control of any relevant person;
- is falling into bad associations or is exposed to moral danger;
- is likely – i) to suffer unnecessarily; or ii) be impaired seriously in his health or development;

due to a lack of parental care;

    a is a child in respect of whom any of the offences mentioned in Schedule 1 to the Criminal Procedure (Scotland) Act 1975 has been committed;

    b is, or is likely to become, a member of the same household as a child in respect of whom any offences mentioned in Schedule 1 to the Criminal Procedure (Scotland) Act 1975 has been committed;

c   is, or is likely to become, a member of the same household as a person who has committed any of the offences mentioned in Schedule 1 to the Criminal Procedure (Scotland) Act 1975;

d   is, or is likely to become, a member of the same household as a person in respect of whom an offence under Section 2A to 2C of the Sexual Offences (Scotland) Act 1976 (incest and intercourse with a child by a step-parent or person in position of trust) has been committed by a member of that household;

e   has failed to attend school regularly without reasonable excuse;

f   has committed an offence*;

g   has misused alcohol or any drug, whether or not a controlled drug within the meaning of the Misuse of Drugs Act 1971;

h   has misused a volatile substance by deliberately inhaling its vapour, other than for a medical purpose;

i   is being provided with accommodation by a local authority under Section 25, or is the subject of a parental responsibilities order obtained under Section 86 of the Act and, in either case, his behaviour is such that special measures are necessary for his adequate supervision in his interest or the interest of others.

Information about the Scottish Children's Hearing System is available on the website of the Scottish Executive (http://www.scotland.gov.uk/).

---

*There are a small number of children, who commit serious offences, who are still dealt with in court.

Index